O9-ABG-412

HOW TO ASSESS
AUTHENTIC LEARNING

4th Edition

Kay Burke

CORWIN PRESS
A SAGE Publications Company
Thousand Oaks, California

Copyright © 2005 by Corwin Press

All rights reserved. When forms and sample documents are included, their use is authorized only by educators, local school sites, and/or noncommercial or nonprofit entities who have purchased the book. Except for that usage, no part of this book may be reproduced or utilized in any form or by any means, electronic or mechanical, including photocopying, recording, or by any information storage and retrieval system, without permission in writing from the publisher.

For information:

Corwin Press
A Sage Publications Company
2455 Teller Road
Thousand Oaks, California 91320
www.corwinpress.com

Sage Publications Ltd.
1 Oliver's Yard
55 City Road
London EC1Y 1SP
United Kingdom

Sage Publications India Pvt. Ltd.
B-42, Panchsheel Enclave
New Delhi 110 017   India

Printed in the United States of America

LCCN 2005921805
ISBN 978-1-5751-7940-7

This book is printed on acid-free paper.

07 08 09 10 9 8 7 6 5 4 3

DEDICATION

To Frank . . .

In the big rubric of life, you have "exceeded expectations" for 35 years.

CONTENTS

Acknowledgements

When I moved from Atlanta to Chicago in 1990, Jim Bellanca, the president of IRI Group in Palatine, interviewed me for a part-time position working with graduate programs. Even though I had been teaching for 20 years and felt confident about teaching language arts, I was embarking on a new career in staff development. It wasn't long before Jim Bellanca and Robin Fogarty introduced me to the wonderful world of multiple intelligences, integrated curricula, cooperative learning, metacognition, transfer, and authentic assessment. Over the next 14 years, the company's name changed from IRI/SkyLight to SkyLight Training and Publishing to Pearson Professional Development to LessonLab. Despite the many changes of strategic plans and people, I will never forget the excitement of the early years when Jim and Robin led a think tank of authors and consultants that included David Lazear, Terry Stirling, Carolyn Chapman, Bruce Williams, Sue Marcus, Beth Swartz, Meir Ben-Hur, Valerie Gregory, Eleanor Rene Rodriquez, Susan Belgrad, Donna Wilson, and many others, all under the watchful eye of our caretaker, Mary Jane Bloethner.

Over the years, the publishing department at SkyLight has also changed. I want to thank Robin Fogarty, Julie Noblitt, Ela Aktay, and Chris Jaeggi for their editorial guidance. The publication team of Donna Ramirez, Bruce Leckie, Heidi Ray, Bob Crump, Dave Stockman, Christina Georgi, and the editorial team of Sue Schumer, Jean Ward, Anne Kaske, Amy Kinsman, and Jodi Keller never cease to amaze me with their professionalism and creativity. I also want to thank Elaine and David Brownlow for their efforts to publish the SkyLight books in Australia and promote quality professional development through their conferences and their passion for helping educators and kids.

I am forever indebted to the thousands of educators I have trained who continue to motivate me with their new ideas. I want to thank my colleagues in Cobb and Muscogee counties, and especially my friends in Fulton County, Georgia, for allowing me to work with their teachers and include some of their checklists in this book.

A special thanks goes to Iris Moran, Randee Nagler, Margaret Pupillo, Ronnie Wade, Maria Balbed, Dee Taylor, Noris Price, Lynn Pennington in Fulton County, and Carol Luitjens, John Nolan, and Amy Erickson with LessonLab, among many others who have supported my efforts to help teachers develop more meaningful assessments for their students.

I will be forever grateful to the principals and teachers in the assessment cadres, the Centennial/Northview/Chattahoochee Cluster, the Tri-Cities Banneker Cluster, and the North Springs Cluster, in Fulton County for their enthusiasm and expertise throughout our assessment training. The performance task portfolios they created set the standard for exceeding expectations.

On a personal note, I want to thank Chris Jaeggi, Susan Gray, and the Maloney IT Team (Danny, Stacie, and Olivia) for all their help and support. I am grateful that my husband Frank, my mother Lois, my sister Carol, and my brothers Mike, Terry, and Jeff pretend to read my books. They humor me by using the word "rubric" during family celebrations. In the words of the 1970s philosopher/songstress Carole King, "My life has been a tapestry . . . A wondrous, woven magic in bits of blue and gold; a tapestry to feel and see, impossible to hold! I know my life is richer for having worked with all of you, and I hope we will continue to touch each other's lives as we weave our own new threads in the tapestry of life.

Thank you.

Kay Burke,
March 2005

Preface

"My life has been a tapestry of rich and royal hue: An everlasting vision of the ever-changing view."—Carole King, 1971

Singer and composer Carole King sang these words on her song and album *Tapestry,* first released in 1971. The album became a best-seller during my first year of teaching ninth grade English at Stranahan High School in Fort Lauderdale, Florida. Many things have changed in 34 years. For one thing, many young people might not know what an "album" is in today's high-tech world of compact disks, iPods®, and Internet downloads! Another thing that has changed is how we assess our students. Throughout my teaching career, I struggled with the "grading issue." I loved assigning creative projects to my high school students. I enjoyed the speeches and skits they presented and I encouraged them to "think outside the box" and try new things.

I can still remember the day I realized that I did not feel comfortable assigning grades to these open-ended subjective assignments. I knew how to grade their writing and grammar because after all, I was a certified Language Arts teacher. But I did not know how to assess their projects and performances. It was a Friday afternoon at Redan High School in Stone Mountain, Georgia. I gazed around my classroom at 75 world literature posters hanging on my walls. Some of the students had produced colorful posters of authors and their works that included quotes, graphics, and pictures that captured the essence of the authors' work beautifully. Others, however, whipped up something in homeroom or between classes. I was overwhelmed by how I was going to assign grades. Should I give them all As for effort? Should I give extra credit or bonus points? It was evident that some of their work was vastly superior to the others, but how could I take off points if I had never told them what I expected?

That day marked a watershed event in my professional life because I realized that if I wanted my students to give me quality work, I needed to provide them the criteria for quality work—*before* they submitted the work. The traditional ways of giving points, using scantron machines to grade multiple choice tests, and "surprising" students with my criteria for grading after they turned in their projects did not work with open-ended, subjective performances. Traditional grading had been an "everlasting vision" in schools, but we were entering a new era of "an ever-changing view" of assessment and evaluation.

One of my professional goals has been to help educators develop more meaningful performance assessments linked to their curriculum goals and state standards. These authentic assessments not only help students produce quality work that meets or exceeds expectations but also help teachers meet the individual learning needs of each student. Throughout the past 15 years, my life has been a tapestry that weaves best practices with the expert advice from my mentors, Jim Bellanca and Robin Fogarty, as well as with the research and input from thousands of teachers, staff developers, administrators, and students in the United States, Canada, and Australia. Together we have created and revised meaningful performance tasks, criteria checklists, scoring rubrics, journals, and teacher-made tests that measure knowledge, performance, and conceptual understanding to help prepare students for a successful life.

I hope this fourth edition of this book that was first published in 1993 will help you continue the journey by helping students become independent thinkers who can internalize the criteria for excellence. Our goal is to have all students become self-directed learners and critical thinkers. The last quote in the conclusion of this book is one of my favorites. Art Costa and Ben Kallick (1992) summarize in two sentences the main purpose of assessment and evaluation. "We must constantly remind ourselves that the ultimate purpose of evaluation is to have students become self-evaluating. If students graduate from our schools still dependent upon others to tell them when they are adequate, good, or excellent, then we've missed the whole point of what education is about" (p. 280).

Thank you for continuing the journey to weave a tapestry of meaningful assessments that will enrich the lives of our students. We can see the grades students earn, but we cannot fully realize the depth of understanding they take away from our classroom. Carole King rereleased *Tapestry* in 1999 with a few new songs. Of course, I bought the new CD to replace the old scratched album. Assessment can be compared to "A tapestry to feel and see, impossible to hold." Sometimes, essential understanding and the love of learning is impossible to feel or see or measure, but at least we should be constantly striving to accept the challenge of the "everlasting vision of the ever-changing view."

Thanks for sharing the vision.

Kay Burke,
March 2005

Introduction

"Assessment is authentic when we anchor testing in the kind of work real people do, rather than merely eliciting easy-to-score responses to simple questions. Authentic assessment is true assessment of performance *because we thereby learn whether students can intelligently use what they have learned in situations that increasingly approximate adult situations, and whether they can innovate new situations."*

—WIGGINS, 1998, p. 21

Authentic assessment is the true assessment of performance.

For many years, assessment has been relegated to a secondary role in the educational process. Many educators feel it has been ignored, misused, and totally misunderstood by administrators, teachers, parents, and students. In the last decade, assessment has emerged as one of the major components in the restructured school. One cannot open an educational journal, attend a workshop, or watch the news without reading and hearing about standards-based reform and high-stakes standardized tests.

The emergence of authentic assessment coincides with an increase in the significance of standardized testing. Almost everyone is aware of the controversy surrounding standardized tests. Charges that high-stakes standardized tests do not always measure significant learner achievement, growth, and development, and do not accurately reflect what students can and cannot do have been made over and over again. Yet, despite the research and the criticism of standardized tests, policymakers, parents, and the general public base much of their perception of the educational system on the publication of standardized test scores and the comparisons of the scores in schools, districts, and states.

Standardized Tests and Classroom Assessments

Standardized Tests

Despite criticisms that standardized tests do not always assess what students are learning and that they emphasize factual knowledge rather then performance or application, they are still the yardstick that the public and policymakers use to measure educational progress. Standardized tests are viewed by many people as being valid and reliable and, for the most part, the most effective method to compare students, schools, districts, states, and nations.

Most people agree that standardized test scores are used to determine many important educational decisions. Some states are using high-stakes standardized tests to promote or retain students, to award diplomas, to reward administrators and teachers with bonuses if their students perform well, and to fire teachers and school administrators or close schools if students perform poorly.

Classroom Assessments

Teachers usually develop most classroom assessments. These assessments consist of a variety of methods including logs, journals, debates, graphic organizers, projects, products, performances, experiments, portfolios, critical or creative writing assignments, skill tests, etc. The purposes of these assessments are to provide feedback to students, evaluate their knowledge and understanding of key concepts and standards, and guide the instructional process. Assessment should be integrated seamlessly with instruction.

Assessment Literacy

Stiggins (1994) discusses the need to develop "assessment literacy" among all the stakeholders concerned about the quality of schools and the achievement of students. He describes assessment literates as those who understand the basic principles of sound assessment and how assessment relates to quality instruction. Teachers must strive to maintain a balanced use of assessment alternatives.

Stiggins says that in the future the educational system will continue to use both standardized testing *and* classroom assessment. "We must appreciate the differences between the two, so as to be able to assure the quality of each" (1994, p. 8). Assessments will continue to provide valuable information for important decision making, but they are also valuable teaching tools that should be used to promote meaningful learning for all students.

Standardized tests are viewed by many people as being valid and reliable.

Introduction

Accountability

The continued lackluster performance of students on national and international tests has become a major political issue. Since the advent of George W. Bush's administration in 2001, the focus of attention moved from standards to school accountability. Solomon (2002) explains that "accountability also implies sanctions for school failure or lack of progress. This makes the assessment high stakes" (p. 25). The *No Child Left Behind Act*, signed on January 8, 2002, calls for mandated testing every year in grades three to eight, to be implemented by the school year 2005–2006, and outlines consequences for schools that do not meet the requirement of value-added progress (comparing scores from year to year) (Solomon, 2002). President George W. Bush also advocates more testing at the high school level.

Grades can affect the self-confidence, self-esteem, motivation, and future of a student.

Elmore (2002) believes that accountability in education today refers to systems that hold students, schools, or districts responsible for academic performance. "Unfortunately, schools and school systems were not designed to respond to the pressure for performance that standards and accountability bring, and their failure to translate this pressure into useful and fulfilling work for students and adults is dangerous to the future of public education" (p. 3).

Grading

Grades are, unfortunately, an integral part of the American educational system. As early as kindergarten, students receive grades that they might not understand. Ask any teacher what he or she hates most about teaching, and there is a good chance his or her answer is "giving grades." Many a teacher has agonized over report cards, trying to decide the fate of a student. It is a gut-wrenching task for teachers to translate everything they know about what a student knows, can do, and feels into one single letter or numerical score. That final grade may determine promotion or retention. It may determine placement in a class or school or participation in extracurricular activities. It may determine school honor roll, class ranking, college admission, college scholarship, or career placement. Currently in some states, such as Georgia and Louisiana, a student's average could prevent that individual from obtaining a scholarship for four years at a state university. Grades are high stakes for students and their families. Many important decisions are made on the basis of a grading system that can be inconsistent, arbitrary, and sometimes punitive.

Grades affect the self-confidence, self-esteem, motivation, and future of a student. Fortunately, some school systems are moving away from traditional letter and number grades at the primary level and adopting performance indicators developed from the standards on report cards. They are also using portfolios, student-led parent-teacher conferences, anecdotal records, checklists, multiple scores, and other more authentic descriptors of students' progress. But despite attempts to restructure report cards to reflect the emphasis on performance, standards, thinking skills, and other indicators, traditional As, Bs, Cs, Ds, and Fs are still used to pass judgment on students.

With the stroke of a pen or the "bubble" of a Scantron computer sheet, a teacher can pass judgment on a student. "It [a grade] marks the lives of those who receive it. It may not be imprinted on the forehead, but it certainly leaves an impression" (Majesky, 1993, p. 88). The grade can become the scarlet letter of Puritan days—especially if it is based on trivial tasks or inappropriate behavior, absences, attitude, and punctuality. "As at the last judgment, students are sorted into the wheat and the chaff. Rewards of As and Bs go out to the good, and punishments of Fs are doled out to the bad. 'Gifts' of Ds (Ds are always gifts) are meted out, and Cs (that wonderfully tepid grade) are bestowed on those whose names teachers can rarely remember" (Majesky, 1993, p. 88).

Grading is a complicated issue and one that must be addressed since grades are used for accountability.

Grading is a complicated issue and one that must be addressed since grades are used for accountability. Airasian (1994) says that grading means "making a judgment about the quality of a pupil's performance, whether it is a performance on a single assessment or performance across many assessments" (p. 281).

O'Connor (2002) says there has been a shift in thinking about assessment. He cites the publication of *Breaking Ranks,* the analysis of secondary schools published by the National Association of Secondary School Principals in 1996 as Summarizing the Shift in Thinking about Assessment. "Teachers will integrate assessment into instruction so that assessment does not merely measure students, but becomes part of the learning process itself" (O'Connor, 2002, p. 25).

Traditional Cognitive Science

The methods of assessment used in schools are often determined by beliefs about learning. Early theories of learning indicated that educators needed to use a "building-blocks-of-knowledge" approach whereby students acquired complex higher-order skills by breaking down learning into a series of skills. Every skill had a prerequisite skill, and it was assumed that after the basic skills were learned, they could be assembled into more complex thinking and

Introduction

insight. Therefore, students who scored poorly on standardized tests at an early age would usually be assigned to the remedial or basic skills classes so they could master those essential basic skills before being exposed to the more challenging and motivating complex thinking skills.

Popham (2001), however, believes that incessant "skill and drill" often turns into "drill and kill." He believes that repetitious instructional activities tend to deaden student's genuine interest in learning. "All the excitement and intellectual vibrancy that students might encounter during a really interesting lesson are driven out by a tedious, test-fostered series of drills" (p. 20.) Moreover, some students choose to drop out of schools rather than sit through tedious lessons and try to pass high-stakes tests to pass a grade or graduate.

Meaningful learning does not just "happen" when students receive information through direct instruction.

Constructivist Theories of Learning

In the constructivist's view, "learning is a constructive process in which the learner is building an internal representation of knowledge, a personal interpretation of experience. This representation is constantly open to change . . . Learning is an active process in which meaning is developed on the basis of experience" (Bednar, Cunningham, Duffy, and Perry, 1993, p. 5).

Constructivists suggest that learning is not linear. It does not occur on a timeline of basic skills. Instead, learning occurs at a very uneven pace and proceeds in many different directions at once. The constructivists also believe that instead of learning being "decontextualized" and taught, for example, by memorizing the parts of speech, it must be situated in a rich context of writing or speaking. Real-world contexts are needed if learning is to be constructed and transferred beyond the classroom. "Many students struggle to understand concepts in isolation, to learn parts without seeing wholes, to make connections where they see only disparity. . . For a good many students, success in school has very little to do with true understanding, and much to do with the concept of curriculum" (Brooks and Brooks, 1993, p. 7).

Meaningful learning does not just "happen" when students receive information through direct instruction. In order for meaningful learning to take place, students must interpret information and relate it to their own prior knowledge. They need to not only know how to perform, but also when to perform and how to change the performance to fit new and different situations (North Central Regional Educational Laboratory [NCREL], 1991b). Therefore, traditional forms of evaluations such as multiple-choice tests assess recall of factual information and one or two of the multiple intelligences.

These tests are rarely able to assess whether or not students can organize complex problems. The new cognitive perspective stresses that meaningful learning is constructive. Learners should be able to construct meaning for themselves, reflect on the significance of the meaning, and self-assess to determine their own strengths and weaknesses. Integrated curricula, cooperative learning, and problem-based learning are just a few examples of curricula that help students construct knowledge for themselves using their multiple intelligences.

Assessments, therefore, should focus on students' acquisition of knowledge, as well as the disposition to use skills and strategies and apply them appropriately. Recent studies suggest that poor thinkers and problem solvers may possess the skills they need, but may fail to use them in certain tasks. Integration of learning, motivation, collaboration, the affective domain, and metacognitive skills all contribute to lifelong learning. Assessment practices must stop measuring knowledge skills and start measuring the disposition to use the skills (NCREL, 1991b).

Assessments should focus on students acquiring knowledge, as well as acquiring the disposition to use skills and strategies and apply them appropriately.

Brain Research

Brain research is a growing field and educators are rushing to implement strategies in what is being called a brain-based classroom. As Wolfe and Brandt (1998) warn, however, "brain research does not—and may never—tell us specifically what we should do in a classroom. At this point it does not 'prove' that a particular strategy will increase student understanding" (p. 8). Educators have a vast background about teaching and learning gained from years of educational research, classroom experience, and cognitive science. Many of the new findings by neuroscientists merely validate some well-established and long accepted theories about educational practice.

Marion Diamond and her colleagues at the University of California at Berkeley pioneered research in the mid-1960s that established the concept of "neural plasticity"—the brain's ability to constantly change its structure and function in response to external experiences. The research team also found that the connections between brain cells—dendrites—can grow at any age. "Our environment, including the classroom environment, is not a neutral place. We educators are either growing dendrites or letting them wither and die. The trick is to determine what constitutes an enriched environment" (Wolfe and Brandt, 1998, p. 11).

Introduction

Fogarty (2002) describes an enriched environment as having "a variety of rich sensory and language experiences that literally stimulate a profusion of dendritic growth" (p. 26).

The classroom environment can be enriched through:

- interaction with others;
- appropriate play materials;
- student choice;
- a pleasant atmosphere; and
- challenging learning experiences (Diamond and Hopson, 1998, pp. 107–108, as cited in Wolfe and Brandt, 1998).

Authentic academic achievement is a prerequisite to authentic assessment.

Students who are involved in meaningful projects and performances are part of an enriched environment. They have choices in determining some of what is included in their portfolios and, most importantly, are active participants in designing the checklists and rubrics by which they will be assessed. A balanced assessment plan implements a wide variety of novel challenges that measure students' growth and development of a wide range of skills that involves the whole child—mentally, physically, aesthetically, socially, and emotionally. The enriched environment provides an enjoyable atmosphere that promotes exploration and the fun of learning.

Authentic Achievement

Archbald and Newmann (1988) believe that before educators try to assess authentically, they should make sure they teach authentically. Authentic academic achievement is a prerequisite to authentic assessment. Archbald and Newmann maintain that achievement tasks should meet at least three criteria: disciplined inquiry, integration of knowledge, and value beyond evaluation.

Disciplined inquiry depends on prior knowledge, an in-depth understanding of a problem, and a move beyond knowledge produced by others to a formulation of new ideas. For example, history students should be able to use primary sources to research generalizations made in their textbooks so that they might be able to form their own conclusions. Science students can develop, perform, and report on their experiments. Through disciplined inquiry methods, students can respond to and sometimes even reject the public knowledge base.

Integration of knowledge requires students to consider things as "whole" rather than as fragments or "factoids." Tests often measure students' knowledge of unrelated facts, definitions, or events. Students may memorize the short answers, but they may not see the whole picture. For example, knowing all the parts of a sentence does not mean one can write a sentence. Archbald and Newmann believe that students "must also be involved in the production, not simply the reproduction, of new knowledge, because this requires knowledge integration" (1988, p. 3). Authentic classroom tasks, therefore, prepare students for life, not just a test.

Archbald and Newmann's final criterion is that authentic achievement must have value beyond evaluation. "When people write letters, news articles, insurance claims, poems; when they speak a foreign language; when they develop blueprints; when they create a painting, a piece of music, or build a stereo cabinet, they demonstrate achievements that have a special value missing in tasks contrived only for the purpose of assessing knowledge (such as spelling quizzes, laboratory exercises, or typical final exams)" (p. 3).

Archbald and Newmann believe that it is important that assigned tasks have some value outside of the classroom. If students are to apply the in-school tasks to life, they first need to perform or produce the skills in school. They also need "flexible time" because the real world does not force people to produce or solve problems by the end of a 50-minute class period. Bell schedules may help manage large numbers of teenagers, but it does not help students learn. Many school systems are moving to block schedules and flexible hours to allow students more time to focus on authentic tasks as well as more time to reflect on their learning.

Another factor necessary for achieving authentic teaching and learning is collaboration. Even though some teachers focus on students working alone, many employers in the business world encourage people to interact and work in teams. Denying students the right to cooperate and collaborate diminishes the authenticity of the achievement. Unless there are some fundamental changes in the nature of schooling itself, students will not see the connection between school and their own lives. They may not realize the interpersonal skills and emotional intelligence necessary to become successful in their careers and in their personal relationships.

Equally important for authentic achievement is a reexamination of the curriculum and the content standards. In this age of information explosion, it is impossible to "cover the curriculum" because there are too many facts and too much material. Instead of allowing students to interact with students

Unless there are some fundamental changes in the nature of schooling itself, students will not see the connection between school and their own lives.

Introduction

and process information, teachers are tackling too much information too superficially. Educators need to practice what Costa calls "selective abandonment" by eliminating the trivial and prioritizing essential learning standards. "Less is more" is the advice Gertrude Stein supposedly gave a young Ernest Hemingway. Educators must ask themselves: What is really important for our students to know today and still use 25 years from now?

Assessment and Evaluation

Assessment is the ongoing process of gathering and analyzing evidence of what a student can do. Evaluation is the process of interpreting the evidence and making judgments and decisions based on the evidence. If the assessment is not sound, the evaluation will not be sound. In most classrooms, teachers assess a student on the basis of observations, conversations, and written work. They make instructional decisions based on these assessments. If the assessment is ongoing and frequent, changes can be made immediately to help the student achieve the desired outcome. If the assessment is flawed, the final evaluation will be based upon invalid and unreliable data. The quality of the final evaluation is only as valid as the ongoing assessment data upon which it is based.

The quality of the final evaluation is only as valid as the ongoing assessment data on which it is based.

Jeroski (1992) maintains that "evaluation is much more than a way of monitoring change—it is the single most powerful way in which teachers communicate their values and beliefs to students, parents, and colleagues. The way we look at evaluation is connected to the way we look at and interact with the world around us" (p. 281).

Since what a student knows is always changing, assessment of what a student knows should be based on comparisons taken over a period of time. The purposes of assessment are many. Policymakers use assessment to set standards, monitor the quality of education, and formulate policies. Administrators use assessment to monitor the effectiveness of a program, identify program strengths and weaknesses, and designate priorities. Teachers use assessment to make grouping decisions, diagnose strengths and weaknesses, evaluate curriculum, give feedback, and determine grades. Parents and students use assessment to gauge student progress and make informed decisions about college and careers (NCREL, 1991b).

Assessment	Evaluation
• Ongoing • Collection of data • Formative	• Final judgment • End result • Summative
Authentic Assessment • Meaningful tasks • Self-assessment • Application	**Portfolio** • Collection of evidence • Growth and development • Framework for learning

Diagnostic Evaluation

Diagnostic evaluations are often administered at the beginning of a course, quarter, semester, or year to assess the skills, abilities, interests, levels of achievement, or difficulties of one student or a class. Diagnostic evaluations should be done informally and are not included in the grade. Teachers can use the results to modify programs, determine causes of learning difficulties, and ascertain students' learning levels. By having information about the student's entry-level skills, a teacher can assess how far the student has progressed throughout the course or year (Board of Education for the City of Etobicoke, 1987). Diagnostic assessments can also be used as baseline data to find out where the students are before a teacher tries a new intervention to produce desired results. Diagnostic tools include items such as pre-tests, writing samples, problem-solving exercises, skill tests, attitude surveys, or questionnaires.

Tomlinson (1999) discusses the strategy of "compacting" where teachers assess students before beginning a unit of study or development of a skill. Students who do well on the preassessment should not have to continue to work on what they already know. Teachers can use a three-stage compacting procedure:

1. Document what the student already knows.
2. Determine what the student does not know and create a plan for how the student will learn those things.
3. Devise meaningful and challenging activities that the student can "buy" if she already knows much about the topic or skill (pp. 91–92).

> **Teachers can use the results of diagnostic evaluations to modify programs and determine causes of learning difficulties.**

Introduction

Formative Evaluation

Formative or ongoing assessments are conducted continually throughout the year. They are used to monitor students' progress and provide meaningful and immediate feedback as to what students have to do to achieve learning standards. Their purpose is to improve instruction throughout the course. Too much emphasis has been placed on the summative or end evaluation where it is discovered what the student does and doesn't know—often too late to do anything about it. Testing has always been separate from learning. Instead, assessment should be an integral part of the learning process—an ongoing part. The results of the formative assessment can be used to redirect efforts, provide information, evaluate the program, and form the basis for the final summative evaluation (Board of Education for the City of Etobicoke, 1987).

Assessment should be an integral part of the learning process—an ongoing part.

"The concept that testing is initiated externally from the student, separate from the learning process, and primarily aimed at determining whether inert knowledge is in students' short-term memories exercises far too much influence over school people today. The goals of thoughtfulness are that students internalize capacities to evaluate their learning, do so as they learn, and do so in ways that exhibit their capacity to be performing thinkers, problem solvers, and inquirers" (Brown, 1989, p. 33).

Summative Evaluation

"Summative evaluation occurs at the end of a unit, activity, course, term or program. It is used with formative evaluation to determine student achievement and program effectiveness" (Board of Education for the City of Etobicoke, 1987, p. 9).

This type of evaluation reports the degree to which course objectives or standards have been met. It can also be used to report to parents, promote or retain, measure student achievement, and measure program effectiveness. Summative evaluation is the "last judgment"—the final grade—the end result. It represents the summation of what the student has learned.

Some Definitions of Authentic Assessment

Many terms or phrases are used when discussing the alternatives to conventional objective or multiple-choice testing. Alternative assessment, authentic assessment, and performance-based assessment are sometimes used synonymously "to mean variants of performance assessments that require students to generate rather than choose a response" (Herman, Aschbacher, and Winters, 1992, p. 2). Stefonek (1991, p. 1) has gathered the following definitions and phrases from experts in the field to describe authentic assessment:

- Methods that emphasize learning and thinking, especially higher-order thinking skills such as problem-solving strategies (Collins)
- Tasks that focus on students' ability to produce a quality product or performance (Wiggins)
- Disciplined inquiry that integrates and produces knowledge, rather than reproduces fragments of information others have discovered (Newmann)
- Meaningful tasks at which students should learn to excel (Wiggins)
- Challenges that require knowledge in good use and good judgment (Wiggins)
- A new type of positive interaction between the assessor and assessee (Wiggins)
- An examination of differences between trivial school tasks (e.g., giving definitions of biological terms) and more meaningful performance in nonschool settings (e.g., completing a field survey of wildlife) (Newmann)
- Involvement that demystifies tasks and standards (Wiggins)

Alternative assessment, authentic assessment, and performance-based assessment are sometimes used synonymously.

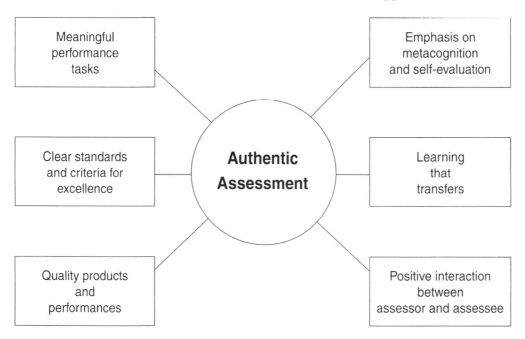

Regardless of the different terminology, most of the various definitions exhibit two central features: "First, all are viewed as alternatives to traditional multiple-choice, standardized achievement tests; second, all refer to direct examination of student performance on significant tasks that are relevant to life outside of school" (Worthen, 1993, p. 445).

Introduction

Archbald and Newmann (1988, p. 1) describe the term *authentic assesment* as follows: "A valid assessment system [that] provides information about the particular tasks on which students succeed or fail, but more important, it also presents tasks that are worthwhile, significant, and meaningful—in short, authentic."

Portfolios

Portfolios allow students to examine their own work and reflect on their learnings.

Portfolios provide collections of student evidence that show students' growth and development over time. Portfolios allow students to examine their own work and reflect on their learnings. They help students analyze their strengths and weaknesses and set both short- and long-term goals. A portfolio contains both formative and summative evaluations because it is a collection of evidence to show how (or if) students are meeting goals or standards.

Accountability Testing

In addition to the assessments created and evaluated by teachers in the classroom, many states are implementing large-scale accountability testing that includes traditional standardized tests as well as some of the new performance-based standardized tests created by testing services and agencies.

Cole describes the differences between measurements developed to assess accountability and policy goals and measurements designed to assess instruction:

Large-Scale Assessment to Serve Accountability and Policy Goals	Classroom Assessment to Support Instruction
1. Formal	1. Informal
2. Objective	2. Teacher-mandated
3. Time-efficient	3. Adapted to local content
4. Cost-effective	4. Locally scored
5. Widely applicable	5. Sensitive to short-term change in students' knowledge
6. Centrally processed	6. Meaningful to students
	7. Immediate and detailed feedback
	8. Tasks that have instructional value
	9. Conducted in a climate of greater trust than standardized tests

(Adapted from Cole as cited in Shephard, 1989, p. 7.)

Some experts worry that the new accountability tests may be oversold and the public will judge the success of teachers and schools solely on the basis of one test! O'Neil (1992) states that testing officials must also decide if state assessment programs can use the tests for accountability purposes as well as for improvement of classroom instruction.

Classroom assessments are usually conducted in a climate of greater trust and relaxation than standardized tests. Classroom observations and grades often do not have to meet the same standards of accuracy. "Errors made in judging individual students are less serious and more easily redressed as teachers gather new evidence. Although single teacher tests are probably less reliable (in a statistical sense) than a one-hour standardized test, accumulation of data gathered about individual pupils in the course of a school year has much more accuracy" (Shepard, 1989, p. 7).

Stiggins wonders why it is necessary to make a choice between traditional and standardized tests and performance assessments. "One of the things that troubles me greatly is that we're setting up performance assessments and paper-and-pencil tests against one another. Each test has a contribution to make. We can't throw away any of the tools at our disposal" (cited in O'Neil, 1992, p. 19). Critics of standardized tests want to throw out the baby with the bath water rather than use all the tools available to assess students fairly, accurately, and authentically.

No one assessment tool by itself is capable of producing the quality information needed to make an accurate judgment.

Balanced Assessment

Assessment should not have to generate an "either/or" or a "throw out the baby with the bath water" approach. Most educators agree with Stiggins that educators need all the tools at their disposal. Shulman (1988) talks about teacher assessment where he suggests educators create "a union of insufficiencies" in which various methods of assessment are combined in such a way that the strengths of one offset the limitations of the other.

Student assessment should follow the same guidelines. No one assessment tool by itself is capable of producing the quality information that is needed to make an accurate judgment of a student's knowledge, skills, understanding of curriculum, motivation, social skills, processing skills, and lifelong learning skills. Each single measurement by itself is insufficient to provide a true portrait of the student or learner. If educators combine standardized and teacher-made tests to measure knowledge and content with portfolios to measure process and growth, and with performances to measure application,

Introduction

the "union of insufficiencies" will indeed provide a more accurate portrait of the individual learner.

Balanced Assessment

Type of Assessment	Focus	Features
Traditional	• Knowledge • Curriculum • Skills	Classroom assessments • Tests • Quizzes • Assignments Standardized tests • Norm-referenced • Criterion-referenced
Portfolio	• Process • Product • Growth	• Growth and development • Reflection • Goal setting • Self-evaluation
Performance	• Standards • Application • Transfer	• Collaboration • Tasks • Criteria • Rubrics • Examination of student work

(Adapted from Fogarty and Stoehr, 1996, p. 198.)

And Now . . . the Tools!

Authentic classroom assessments provide teachers with a repertoire, a vast array of tools to measure student growth. The following chapters focus on specific tools teachers need to create a vivid, colorful, and true portrait of a student as he or she develops and grows over the course of a year. In the past, a student's progress was chronicled by a superficial "snapshot" of the student. The snapshot usually consisted of a few pictures of standardized test scores, midterms, final grades, and other one-dimensional scores that lay lifeless in the permanent record file.

The grades on the report card do not adequately describe the skills the students had when they entered a class, as compared to the skills they had when they left the class. Nothing more than a static glimpse of a student can be gleaned from the traditional cumulative record system that has dominated our school systems the past two centuries.

A more vivid image of the student of the twenty-first century is emerging in the authentic classroom. Instead of a flat, one-dimensional "picture" in a folder, teachers can capture the vitality, movement, and physical and mental growth of a student in an interactive "video."

The "video" is colorful, alive, and fluid. One can see students develop, change, and grow in every frame. And what's more important is that students can see themselves develop, change, and grow. At the end of the year, parents, teachers, and students can review this growth and development of the students and set new goals.

Each chapter in this book will introduce a tool to "videotape" a student's growth and achievement. The chapters include a description of *what* the tool is, *why* we should use the tool, and *how* we should use the tool. Examples of many of the assessments are provided, and teachers will get a chance to create original tools on the On Your Own page at the end of each chapter, as well as self-evaluate their work on the Reflection page. *How to Assess Authentic Learning* presents only a few of the many options available for teachers to add to their repertoire of assessment strategies. As educators review the strategies in this book, they turn on the "power," push the "play" button, and prepare to "videotape" a student in motion—a student of the twenty-first century.

Authentic classroom assessments provide teachers with a repertoire, a vast array of tools to measure student growth.

Introduction

Cathy reviews, self-evaluates, and reflects on her own video performances as she plans for her future.

STUDENT LEARNING STANDARDS

CHAPTER 1

"Standards can improve achievement by clearly defining what is to be taught and what kind of performance is expected."

—RAVITCH, 1995, P. 25

Student Learning Standards

What Are Student Learning Standards?

Standards clarify expectations and consensus about what constitutes quality products and practice.

"The use of the term *standards* instead of the traditional educator's term *objectives* foreshadowed a strengthening of government's determination and role in school administration. Both terms essentially entail a process of coming to consensus and explicit statements of the elements of the American culture worthy of transmission. In this respect, the standards parallel traditional goals and objectives as well as outcomes. The term *standard*, however, has an implication of high levels of expectations and monitoring that were not commonly connected to the widely used educational objectives suggested by Tyler (1949) as clarified statements of school curriculum" (Solomon, 2002, p. 22).

Most educators attribute the publication of *A Nation at Risk* (National Commission on Excellence in Education) in 1983 as the impetus for setting standards at a national level. The concern over education was also the focus of the first education summit, held in Charlottesville, Virginia, in September 1989, where the nation's fifty governors and President George H. W. Bush adopted national educational goals for the year 2000. One of the goals was to establish challenging national achievement standards for five school subjects—English, mathematics, science, history, and geography. As a result of the summit, a number of national organizations representing various subject areas published numerous documents (Marzano and Kendall, 1996).

Diane Ravitch, former Assistant Secretary of Education, is recognized as one of the chief proponents of the standards movement. Ravitch wrote the book *National Standards in American Education: A Citizen's Guide* (1995), in which she explains the rationale for standards: "Americans . . . expect strict standards to govern construction of buildings, bridges, highways, and tunnels; shabby work would put lives at risk. They expect stringent standards to protect their drinking water, the food they eat, and the air they breathe . . . standards are created because they improve the quality of life" (Ravitch, 1995, cited in Marzano and Kendall, 1996, p. 1).

Darling-Hammond (1997), in her book *The Right to Learn,* agrees that standards of practice are used to license professionals and guide the work of architects in constructing sound buildings, accountants in managing finances, engineers in assembling space shuttles, and doctors in treating patients. She adds, however, "These standards are not prescriptions; instead they reflect shared norms and knowledge about underlying principles of practice, the effects of various techniques, and decision-making processes"

(p. 213). Standards, therefore, clarify expectations and consensus about what constitutes quality products and practice.

Wiggins (1998) believes that a true standard describes a specific and desirable level of exemplary performance. He says it should be "a worthwhile target irrespective of whether most people can meet it at the moment" (p. 105). In addition, students should be able to internalize their own standards of quality work. Brooks (2002) believes that "the most influential parents, teachers, and supervisors are the ones who know how to help those who seek guidance *set their own standards,* or, at least, adopt, agree with, or see the merit in a published set of standards" (p. 3).

National Standards

Standard-setting efforts have been undertaken by a number of national organizations representing various subject areas as well as the United States Department of Education. The documents published by such organizations as the National Council of Teachers of English (NCTE) and the National Council of Teachers of Mathematics (NCTM) offer their versions of standards in their subject areas.

Many of these standards documents vary because of the differing definitions of standards. Some standards are very general, such as "understanding the arts in relation to history and cultures" proposed by the *National Standards for Arts Education,* 1994; other standards are more specific, such as "students should understand the causes of the Civil War" as proposed in the *National Standards for United States History: Exploring the American Experience* (Marzano and Kendall, 1996, p. 22). In addition to the wide variance in the specificity of standards, Marzano and Kendall describe the problem of "varying levels of subordination," in which some standards have a complex structure in terms of subordination (topic, understandings, elements, components, example of student achievement) and others, as shown below, map out a general area and then provide benchmarks that describe appropriate expectations at specific grade levels.

Mathematics content standard: The student demonstrates number sense and an understanding of number theory.

- *Middle school benchmark:* The student understands the relationship of decimals to whole numbers.
- *High school benchmark:* The student understands the characteristics of the real number system and its subsystems. (Marzano and Kendall, 1996, pp. 24–25)

Students should be able to internalize their own standards of quality work.

Student Learning Standards

Format of Standards

The lack of uniformity in national standards makes it difficult for school districts to adopt the subject-specific national documents for all subject areas and organize their schools around them. Some standards deal with content, while others address curriculum, performance, or lifelong learning skills. This format inconsistency among the various national organizations who have set standards has caused most states, districts, and schools to use the national standards as models to create their own standards, which they construct with the same type of format to allow for more consistent application and assessment. Despite the inconsistency in the format of standards, the basic concepts and key learning components are very similar from state to state. Almost all language arts standards address expectations related to communication skills—reading, writing, speaking, technology. Differences occur when the standards are written as content skills, performance standards, or task (work-design) standards.

Some standards deal with content, while others address curriculum, performance, or lifelong learning skills.

Management Issues

Theorist Elliot Eisner (1995) noted the similarity of the standards movement to the efficiency movement that began in 1913 when Frederick Taylor, the inventor of the time-and-motion study, was hired by industrialists to make plants more efficient and profitable. According to Eisner, school administrators soon found that the basic concept underlying the efficiency movement—routine mechanization of teaching and learning—did not work. Eisner concludes that educators will no doubt come to the same conclusions about standards (cited in Marzano and Kendall, 1996). Many teachers can still remember the 1960s and 1970s, when they had to prepare lesson plans that targeted hundreds of behavioral objectives for each of their students. The paperwork involved in documenting the objectives occupied much of teachers' time, often at the expense of effective teaching and meaningful learning.

Darling-Hammond (1997) is afraid the sheer number of the performance indicators in the new standards documents would create expectations for drill-and-skill "content coverage" at the expense of in-depth understanding and application of key ideas. Strong, Silver, and Perini (2001) feel that standards seem to drain the life out of teaching and learning. They cite recent research by Kendall, Marzano, and Gaddy (1999) that says if teachers attempted to teach to all the standards now in place, the average student would need to add *five* more years to his school career. They say, "Think of a newspaper cartoon where the valedictorian addresses the class by saying, 'Congratulations, fellow high school graduates. We are now in full-possession of a standards-based education. Unfortunately, we're 24'" (p. 94).

Standards have the potential to increase student achievement, but the process of development and implementation must be examined carefully so that learning standards are used to enhance learning, not to create a paperwork management nightmare that drains the life out of teaching and learning.

Types of Standards

Standards pervade education. Some of the most commonly identified standards address the following: *content, performance, lifelong learning, and opportunity to learn.* Almost all standards also contain *benchmarks* or specific performance indicators which represent the specific learning that will be demonstrated by the students at varying levels of their cognitive development.

Content Standards

Content standards refer to knowledge and skills belonging to a particular discipline. The content standards depict the key elements in the program through a focused and clear approach to the subject (Foriska, 1998). Content standards answer the question: What should students know and be able to do? Following are some sample standards:

- *Science standard:* Explain the relationships among science, technology, and society.
- *Physical education standard:* Demonstrate individual development in swimming and water safety.

(Foriska, 1998, p. 49)

The knowledge itself is usually divided into two types: content and process. Content knowledge is classified into a hierarchy ranging from facts about specific persons, places, things, and events to concepts and generalizations. The processes are identified as skills or strategies that can be applied to many types of situations (Marzano, Pickering, and McTighe, 1993, cited in Foriska, 1998, p. 53).

Benchmarks

Following the development of content standards, benchmarks are developed. "Benchmarks detail the progression of reasonable expectations for acquiring the skills and knowledge needed to reach the content standards" (Foriska, 1998, p. 31). The desired student performance related to the benchmark is a key connection for linking assessment and instruction. Benchmarks often target specific grade levels or stages.

The desired student performance related to the benchmark is a key connection for linking assessment and instruction.

Student Learning Standards

Marzano and Kendall (1996) maintain that standards are generally broad and contain somewhat arbitrary categories of knowledge. Benchmarks, however, represent the real substance of standards construction. Marzano and Kendall state that benchmarks can be written in three general formats: (1) as statements of information and skills (declarative and procedural); (2) as performance activities; (3) as performance tasks (p. 53).

Foriska (1998) describes benchmarks as the guideposts that "identify a progression of reasonable expectations detailing what students are capable of learning at different ages with regard to the content standards. This makes the structure of the curriculum appropriate for the cognitive development of the students" (pp. 31–32). Benchmarks provide the framework for teaching and assessing key concepts because they are more specific and concrete than most standards.

Benchmarks represent the real substance of standards construction.

A language arts standard from Illinois states that students in middle or junior high should "speak effectively using language appropriate to the situation and audience." The benchmark describes specific criteria related to the standard. These criteria can be developed later into a checklist or rubric for assessment purposes. (See the sample checklist on the next page.)

Performance Standards

Performance standards focus on "students applying and demonstrating what they know and can do while defining the levels of learning that are considered satisfactory." Solomon (2002) says the performance standard is intended as a clearly discriminated level of the bar or model of acceptable performance. The performance standard is a translation of the content standard that additionally provides an expectation level and answers the question, "How good is good enough?" (p. 58).

Rubrics

A common convention to refer to a set of performance levels is a rubric. Rubrics are guidelines that measure degrees of quality. Solomon (2002) writes that a rubric is an assessment tool that verbally describes the scale levels of student achievement on performance tasks. Moreover, "for the purpose of meaningful assessment of student performance, the standards or performance indicators need to be translated into rubrics" (p. 58). See page 19 for an example of a rubric developed from the criteria of the Illinois language arts standard and checklist on p. 7.

Illinois English Language Arts Standard 4.B.:
Speak effectively using language appropriate to the situation and audience.

Middle/Junior High School Benchmark:
Deliver planned oral presentations using language and vocabulary appropriate to the purpose, message, and audience; provide details and supporting information that clarify main ideas; and use visual aids and contemporary technology as support.

ORAL PRESENTATION CHECKLIST CORRELATED TO STANDARDS		
Criteria/Performance Indicators	**Not Yet** 0	**Some Evidence** ✓
Language and Vocabulary		
• Appropriate to the purpose		
• Appropriate to the message		
• Appropriate to the audience		
Information to Support the Main Idea		
• Details		
• Examples		
• Statistics		
• Quotes		
• Anecdotes		
Visual Aids (select at least two)		
• Graphic organizer		
• Picture		
• Poster		
• Prop		
• Pamphlet		
• Costume		
Technology (select two)		
• Transparencies		
• Slides		
• PowerPoint™		
• Videotape		
• Digital pictures		

(Burke, 1999, p. 8)

Student Learning Standards

Lifelong Learning Standards

Lifelong learning standards help students become lifelong learners and are commonly associated with the world of work. Marzano and Kendall (1996) describe how attention was focused on these workplace-related skills in 1991 when the Secretary's Commission on Achieving Necessary Skills (SCANS) published the report *What Work Requires of Schools: A SCANS Report for America 2000*. The commission members spent twelve months talking to business owners and public employees to determine the types of skills that would make students productive members of the workforce.

The SCANS report identified a three-part foundation of skills and personal qualities, as follows:

Lifelong learning standards are commonly associated with the world of work.

- The first part of the foundation involved traditional academic content such as reading, writing, arithmetic, mathematics, speaking, and listening.
- The second part of the foundation involved the thinking skills of thinking creatively, making decisions, solving problems, seeing things in the mind's eye, knowing how to learn, and reasoning.
- The third part of the foundation involved lifelong learning skills, such as individual responsibility, self-esteem, sociability, self-management, and integrity.

(as cited in Marzano and Kendall, 1996, p. 40).

Marzano and Kendall (1996) compiled a comprehensive record of many of the lifelong learning skills identified in national and state documents:

LIFELONG LEARNING SKILLS

Working With Others
1. Contributes to the overall effort of a group.
2. Uses conflict-resolution techniques.
3. Works well with diverse individuals and in diverse situations.
4. Displays effective interpersonal communication skills.
5. Demonstrates leadership skills.

Self-Regulation
1. Sets and manages goals.
2. Performs self-appraisal.
3. Considers risks.
4. Demonstrates perseverance.
5. Maintains a healthy self-concept.
6. Restrains impulsivity.

(Marzano and Kendall, 1996, p. 41. Reprinted with permission.)

Thornburg (2002) feels that "our dynamic world requires flexibility in everything from the school curriculum to the nature of the workplace itself. This means we must be prepared to add new skills to our list as they become apparent" (p. 2).

Opportunity-to-Learn Standards

Opportunity-to-learn standards focus on the conditions and resources necessary to give students an equal chance to achieve standards. When all students are to be held to the same set of learning standards, there must be ways to ensure they have access to all the conditions needed for them to meet those standards. Often legislatures, community members, and state organizations plan punitive measures to punish school districts, principals, teachers, and, sadly, children if they do not meet the standards. Such measures include plain schools on probation or having them taken over by the state; removing principals; penalizing teachers financially; and, having parents obtain vouchers.

Students must be given access to all the conditions needed for them to meet the standards.

Darling-Hammond and Falk (1997) advocate that "along with standards for student learning, school systems should develop 'opportunity-to-learn' standards—standards for delivery systems and standards of practice—to identify how well schools are doing in providing students with the conditions they need to achieve and to trigger corrective actions from the state and district" (p. 196). If learning materials and supplies are not available, appropriate learning activities are not provided, or instruction is poor, students may not have the same opportunities to learn as students who have materials and effective instruction.

Stevens (as cited in Williams, 1996), identified four variables to explain differences in students' academic achievement. These variables were tied principally to the providers of instruction, teachers, and school principals—not to students. The variables are "content coverage, content exposure, content emphasis, and quality of instructional delivery. These variables provide powerful insight into issues of equity and accountability in schools" (p. 79).

Wolk (1998) warns that standards-based school reform is on "a collision course with reality" because states hold accountable and apply sanctions to schools whose students fail to meet standards, despite the fact that "a great many high school and middle school students, especially in urban districts, cannot read well enough to pass these tough courses and tests" (p. 48).

Why Do We Need Standards?

Standards can be a blueprint to ensure that all students are learning the necessary knowledge and skills. "Once there is a clear understanding of what students should learn, effective instructional practices can be designed to teach the standards, and appropriate multiple measures can be developed which are reliable, valid, and fair to ascertain the level at which students are learning the standards" (Ardovino, Hollingsworth, and Ybarra, 2000, p. 90).

Marzano and Kendall (1996), in their book *A Comprehensive Guide to Designing Standards-Based Districts, Schools, and Classrooms,* cite at least four reasons that standards represent one of the most powerful options for school reform:

> **Studies have shown a disparity among teachers concerning the amount of time spent teaching a particular subject area or skill.**

1. Erosion of the Carnegie unit and the common curriculum
2. Variation in current grading practices
3. Lack of attention to educational outputs
4. Competing countries do it

(pp. 11–18, reprinted with permission.)

Erosion of the Carnegie Unit and the Common Curriculum

Veteran educators remember the shift away from the standard concept of credit hours (based on the Carnegie unit—a measure of class time) and proliferation of elective courses in the 1960s and 1970s. It was not unusual for students to elect to take "Science Fiction Short Stories" or "Gothic Mystery Writers" in lieu of American literature or composition. Furthermore, studies have shown a disparity among teachers concerning the amount of time spent teaching a particular subject area or skill. How many teachers have spent six weeks covering the Civil War in a history class, and then not have sufficient time for World War I or II? Because teachers sometimes make arbitrary decisions regarding what they teach, there is often a lack of uniformity in a given district's or state's curricula and little consistency in the knowledge and skills covered within subject areas.

Variation in Current Grading Practices

Grading has always been an ambiguous process. What does a B really mean? How many teachers average effort, behavior, cooperation, and attendance into the academic grade, thus conveying an inaccurate portrayal of a student's achievement? O'Connor (2002) contends it is difficult to know how a teacher arrives at a grade because grades are often imprecise and sometimes are not indicative of what students know and can do in a subject area.

Lack of Attention to Educational Outputs

The outcomes-based education movement attempted to focus attention not so much on the input of instructional delivery but on the outcome of the results. Unfortunately, some of the outcomes were difficult to measure objectively, and some parents felt educators should not be measuring outcomes that included values. Glickman (1993, cited in Schmoker 1996) feels too much emphasis has been placed on new instructional strategies, the innovation, or the "hot topic" rather than on the results for the learner. Having the entire school wired for technology is wonderful. Integrating the theory of multiple intelligences into each lesson is motivating. However, the bottom line should always be: How does it affect student achievement? Today, schools are paying more attention to results, not intentions. The "A" word of the twenty-first century is accountability.

Competing Countries Do It

The fourth reason for implementing standards for school reform addresses the issue of competition with other countries. Proponents of standards often point to countries such as China, Japan, France, and England to show how setting standards and developing a national curriculum, national exams, and cut-off scores can help students attain academic excellence. Many business and community leaders have vigorously supported the establishment of student performance standards to create a world-class workforce. Behind this expectation is the assumption that higher educational standards and student performance are keys to higher workplace productivity (Marzano and Kendall, 1996).

Levin (1998), however, reviewed evidence and found only a weak relationship between test scores and economic productivity and virtually no evidence on the predictive validity of the newer performance standards. He suggests that "the educational standards movement has relied on the economic rationale largely because of its persuasiveness in stimulating educational reform rather than any compelling evidence on the links between specific educational standards and economic performance" (p. 4). Noted labor economist Clark Kerr examined a range of evidence on the contention that education is the key to the nation's competitiveness and concluded, "seldom in the course of policy making in the United States have so many firm convictions held by so many been based on so little proof" (1991, cited in Levin, 1998, p. 5).

The standards movement has gathered momentum on the basis of these four reasons as well as the public's dissatisfaction with the quality of students the public schools are producing. Headlines about scores on international

> The bottom line should always be: How does it affect student achievement?

tests showing the placement of the United States have fueled the groundswell of support for high standards for academic excellence. Moreover, the members of the business community have expressed concern over the skills their employees lack and the inordinate amount of time and money they are spending to teach their employees what they feel they should have learned in public schools. The public seems to support the concept that teachers provide clear and appropriate expectations to students and evaluate their progress accurately.

How Can We Use Standards?

Darling-Hammond (1997, p. 213) advises that standards can be most useful when used as "guideposts not straitjackets."

Many barriers must be overcome in order for a district to implement a standards-based accountability system. Ardovino, Hollingsworth, and Ybarra (2000) found that in many districts the only educators who assert that they have adopted standards are the administrators. Many teachers know where to find them and even know the buzz words—grade-level standards, proficiencies, benchmarks, exemplars, rubrics, and so on. However, "in our experience it is rare for individual teachers to comprehend them in any substantive way or to have assimilated them into the web of daily teaching" (p. 85).

Darling-Hammond (1997) advises that standards can be most useful when used as "guideposts not straitjackets for building curriculum assessments and professional development opportunities, and when they are used to focus and mobilize system resources rather than to punish students and schools" (p. 213).

Standards as Guideposts

When used by administrators, teachers, and parents effectively, standards can target nine important goals:

1 – Synthesize Educational Goals
Educators need to focus on attaining important goals that will benefit all students. Establishing a few clear and specific goals can focus a faculty on developing action plans and unifying efforts to achieve the goals. Schmoker (1996) says, "Goals themselves lead not only to success, but also to the effectiveness and cohesion of a team" (p. 19). Educators need to set goals in their strategic plans in order to later measure their success in meeting the goals.

2 – Target Student Achievement

The primary purpose for standards is to focus attention on student work and improved student achievement. Cohen (1995) states, "It is student work that we want to improve, not standards or scholars' ideas about standards" (p. 755). The emphasis is changing from the "input" of what teachers teach to the "output" of what students learn. Standards are not the end; they are a means to achieve the end—improved student achievement.

STANDARDS AS GUIDEPOSTS

Standards can benefit students by helping educators to:

S ynthesize educational goals

T arget student achievement

A lign curriculum systematically

N otify the public of results

D etermine criteria for quality work

A nalyze data

R efocus instructional methodology

D edicate resources for professional development

S erve the needs of a diverse population

Student Learning Standards

3 – Align Curriculum Systemically

The "erosion of the common curriculum" has caused teachers to pick and choose what they want to teach without always being aware of essential learnings in the subject area. The standards and benchmarks provide guideposts and key concepts that help focus teachers on a relatively small set of core ideas. The curriculum has become so overwhelming, teachers are forced to either cover a great deal of information superficially, or as Costa says, "selectively abandon" their curriculum. Many districts are also working on curriculum mapping to develop a blueprint of not only *what* essential skills are taught, but also *when* they are taught. A curriculum aligned with meaningful standards and authentic assessments is a powerful predictor of increased student achievement.

4 – Notify the Public of Results

One of the reasons the public is demanding standards is because they are concerned about the quality of the schools. Newspaper headlines about how students in the United States compare with students in other countries and the decline of Scholastic Aptitude Test (SAT) scores cause alarm among parents and business leaders. Elmore (2002) states that the accountability movement expresses society's expectation that schools will solve the problems that lead to the academic failure of a large number of students and the mediocre performance of many more. "Failure will lead to erosion of public support and a loss of legitimacy" (p. 3).

5 – Determine Criteria for Quality Work

One of the most important by-products of the standards movement is the emphasis on establishing specific criteria for all student work. Teachers are involving their students in determining the criteria for assignments and the indicators of quality to determine, How good is it? Conversations among teachers, parents, and students about what constitutes "A" work and the creation of checklists and scoring rubrics to guide the students have demystified the grading process. Students know not only the expectations, but also the steps they need to take to meet the expectations. The emphasis on performance assessments helps students internalize the criteria and become critical evaluators of their own work.

6 – Analyze Data

School personnel have found that if they use standards to drive student achievement, they need to measure a school's progress with hard data—something schools have not done well. Schmoker (1996) believes educators fear data because of its capacity to reveal strengths and weaknesses, failures and successes. Harrington-Lueker (1998) maintains that districts engaged in standards-based reform must "routinely analyze data on student

The emphasis on performance assessments helps students internalize the criteria and become critical self-evaluators.

achievement—the number of students completing algebra and geometry, the number enrolled in Advanced Placement classes, the number receiving Ds and Fs and so on" (p. 21). The *No Child Left Behind Act of 2001* calls for mandated testing every year in grades three to eight and a set of consequences should schools not meet the requirement of value-added progress. Data collection and analysis are critical components of standards-based education.

7 – Refocus Instructional Methodology

The most comprehensive standards in the world will not by their very existence improve education. The key to improving student achievement is instruction. In order to meet the needs of a diverse student population, teachers need to integrate a repertoire of instructional strategies to help all students learn. Though the drill-and-skill lecture method may appeal to some parents and students, fewer and fewer students are responding to that mode of instruction. Instructors are utilizing Gardner's multiple intelligences theory to prepare lessons and assessments to address students' learning styles and interests. Other teachers are using cooperative learning techniques, problem-based learning approaches, integrated curricula lessons, and portfolios to promote teamwork, thinking skills, and connections among subject areas. Research on brain-compatible learning provides strategies teachers can implement to enrich the learning environment, foster reflection and self-evaluation, and stimulate student interest in new areas of study. Darling-Hammond (1997) believes real improvement will come about because "the standards come alive when teachers study student work, collaborate with other teachers to improve their understanding of subjects and students' thinking, and develop new approaches to teaching that are relevant and useful for them and their students" (p. 236).

8 – Dedicate Resources for Professional Development

The standards movement goes way beyond standards for students. It takes a dedicated and competent teacher to implement the instructional strategies to help students learn. The statistics about the number of uncertified teachers, especially in the fields of science and mathematics and in urban districts, are staggering. One report shows one-third of mathematics teachers have neither a college major or minor in mathematics, half of all high school physical science teachers don't have any background in any of the physical sciences; and one in five high school English teachers do not have even a minor in English (Messacappa, 1998).

Elmore (2002) feels that if the public and policymakers want increased attention paid to academic quality and performance, they have to invest in the knowledge and skills of educators. He says that "in public schools, there are few portals through which new knowledge about teaching and

Data collection and analysis are critical components of standards-based education.

learning can enter schools; few structures or processes in which teachers and administrators can assimilate, adapt, and polish new ideas and practices; and few sources of assistance for those who are struggling to understand the connection between the academic performance of their students and the practices in which they engage" (p. 5).

9 – Serve the Needs of a Diverse Population

One of the biggest paradoxes of the standards movement is requiring all students to meet the same standards.

One of the biggest paradoxes of the standards movement is requiring all students to meet the same standards, regardless of their reading ability, their socio-economic status, or the quality of their education. Not every student enters school with the same abilities, and Darling-Hammond (1997) says we must allow for "differing starting points and pathways to learning so that students are not left out or left behind" (p. 231). Establishing the standard will not help a student meet the standard. Teachers will have to work with a diverse group of students and experiment with a wide variety of instructional and assessment strategies to see which ones work best. All students may not reach the standard, but they know where they are and what they still need to do. Williams (1996) believes the greatest challenge for urban schools is the issue of low academic achievement. She cites a report *Making Schools Work for Children of Poverty* (1992) that concludes that low expectations and the absence of rigor in urban schools with concentrations of children in poverty "consigns them to lives without the knowledge and skills they need to exist anywhere but on the margins of our society and consigns the rest of us to forever bear the burden of their support" (as cited in Williams, p. 3).

Final Thoughts

Arthur Costa once addressed an audience at an educational conference and asked, "How many of you in the audience are old enough to have been through three back-to-basic movements?" The audience members laughed and nodded their heads. The members of that audience, like so many veteran educators, recognize how many educational movements have come and gone, sometimes sapping the strength and enthusiasm of those involved and making educators somewhat cynical of "innovations" and "systemic reform." New math, transformational grammar, time on task, outcomes-based education, and whole language are just a few of the many educational reforms that have been implemented and, in some cases, abandoned. The standards-based reform movement may continue to drive education in the twenty-first century if all the stakeholders buy into the concept that standards will pull everything together.

According to Ardovino, Hollingsworth, and Ybarra (2000), "The standards movement is about assessing 'what was taught and what was learned.' Educators can no longer be independent contractors with multiple game plans. Standards provide cohesiveness that will certify the content our students are learning" (pp. 90–91).

Student Learning Standards

PRIMARY

MATH

- Uses a variety of strategies in the problem-solving process.
- Understands and applies basic and advanced properties of the concept of numbers.
- Uses basic and advanced procedures while performing the processes of computation.
- Understands and applies basic and advanced properties of the concepts of measurement.
- Understands and applies basic and advanced properties of the concepts of geometry.
- Understands and applies basic and advanced properties of the concepts of statistics and data analysis.
- Understands and applies basic and advanced properties of the concepts of probability.
- Understands and applies basic and advanced properties of the concepts of functions and algebra.
- Understands the general nature and uses of mathematics.

MIDDLE

SCIENCE

Earth and Space

- Understands basic features of the Earth.
- Understands basic Earth processes.
- Understands essential ideas about the composition and structure of the universe and the Earth's place in it.

Life Sciences

- Knows about the diversity and unity that characterize life.
- Understands the genetic basis for the transfer of biological characteristics from one generation to the next.
- Knows the general structure and functions of cells in organisms.
- Understands how species depend on one another and on the environment for survival.
- Understands the cycling of matter and flow of energy throughout the living environment.
- Understands the basic concepts of the evolution of species.

HIGH

LANGUAGE ARTS

Writing

- Demonstrates competence in the general skills and strategies of the writing process.
- Demonstrates competence in the stylistic and rhetorical aspects of writing.
- Uses grammatical and mechanical conventions in written compositions.
- Gathers and uses information for research purposes.

Reading

- Demonstrates competence in the general skills and strategies of the reading process.
- Demonstrates competence in general skills and strategies for reading a variety of literary texts.
- Demonstrates competence in the general skills and strategies for reading a variety of informational texts.

Listening and Speaking

- Demonstrates competence in speaking and listening as tools for learning.

COLLEGE

LIFE SKILLS

Thinking and Reasoning

- Understands and applies basic principles of presenting an argument.
- Understands and applies basic principles of logic and reasoning.
- Effectively uses mental processes that are based on identifying similarities and differences (compares, contrasts, classifies).
- Understands and applies basic principles of hypothesis testing and scientific inquiry.
- Applies basic troubleshooting and problem-solving techniques.
- Applies decision-making techniques.

Working With Others

- Contributes to the overall effort of a group.
- Uses conflict-resolution techniques.
- Works well with diverse individuals and in diverse situations.
- Displays effective interpersonal communication skills.
- Demonstrates leadership skills.

Kendall, J. S., & Marzano, R. J. (1997). *Content Knowledge: A Compendium of Standards and Benchmarks for K–12 Education,* 2nd Edition. Aurora, CO: MCREL and Alexandria, VA: ASCD. Note the above are excerpts from standards lists and are reprinted here by permission of the publisher.

EXAMPLE

Oral Presentation Rubric Correlated to Standards

Illinois Language Arts Standard 4.B.:
Speak effectively using language appropriate to the situation and audience.

Middle Junior High School Benchmark:
Deliver planned oral presentations using language and vocabulary appropriate to the purpose, message, and audience; provide details and supporting information that clarify main ideas; and use visual aids and contemporary technology as support.

Criteria:	Scale: 1 Practiced in Front of Mirror (Novice)	2 Enrolled in Toastmaster Course (In Progress)	3 Voted Class President (Meets Standards)	4 Nominated for an Oscar (Exceeds Standards)
Appropriate Language/Vocabulary				
• Purpose • Message • Audience	• Inappropriate language • Limited vocabulary	Language and vocabulary appropriate to purpose	Language and vocabulary appropriate to the purpose and the message	Language and vocabulary appropriate to the purpose, message, and audience
Information Supports Main Idea				
• Details • Examples • Statistics • Quotes • Anecdotes	Limited use of details to support main idea	Use of: • details • examples	Use of: • details • examples • statistics • quotes	Use of appropriate: • details • examples • statistics • quotes • anecdotes
Visual Aids (Minimum of 2)				
• Graphic organizer • Picture • Poster • Prop • Pamphlet • Costume	No visual aids used in presentation	Use of *one* visual aid to support main idea	Use of *two* visual aids to support main idea and keep the attention of the audience	Use of *two or more* visual aids to support main idea, keep the attention of the audience, and motivate the audience
Technology (Minimum of 2)				
• Transparencies • Slides • PowerPoint™ • Videotape • Digital pictures	No use of technology	Use of *one* technology tool that supports main idea	Use of *two* technology tools to support main idea and keep the attention of the audience	Use of *two or more* contemporary technology tools to clarify main idea and inspire the audience to action

Student Comment:

Teacher Comment:

Total points _____
Scale 15–16 = A
     13–14 = B
     9–12 = C
     1–8 = Not Yet

Student Learning Standards

Rubric Template

Standard: _____

Benchmark: _____

Scale:	1	2	3	4
Criteria:				
•				
•				
•				
•				
•				
•				
•				
•				
•				
•				
•				
•				

Student Learning Standards

1. Review this chapter and other resources on standards, and then discuss your ideas with a colleague. Complete the following graphic describing the advantages and disadvantages of the standards-based movement.

STANDARDS-BASED MOVEMENT

	Advantages	Disadvantages
Example:	• It will help teachers focus their curriculum.	• It could become too prescriptive and uniform.
	•	•
	•	•
	•	•
	•	•
	•	•

2. Summarize your feelings by completing the stem question: When I think of the standards-based movement, I wonder . . .

3. Share your reflection on the standards-based movement with a colleague.

STANDARDIZED TESTS

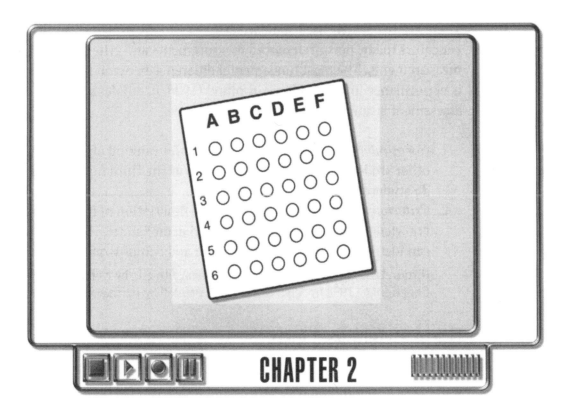

CHAPTER 2

"A standardized test is a test, either norm-referenced or criterion-referenced, that is administered, scored, and interpreted in a standard manner."

—POPHAM, 1999, P. 264

Standardized Tests

What Are Standardized Tests?

Standardized tests are tests that are standardized in four areas. Bracey (1998, p. 17) in *Put to the Test: An Educator's and Consumer's Guide to Standardized Testing* (Phi Delta Kappa International) describes the four as follows:

1. *Format.* The format of all the questions for all the students is the same (usually, but not always, multiple choice).
2. *Questions.* All the questions for all the students are the same.
3. *Instructions.* All the instructions for all students are the same.
4. *Time allotment.* The time permitted to complete the test for all the students is the same.

Standardized tests are tests that are standardized in four areas: format, questions, instructions, and time allotment.

There are two widely used standardized assessment strategies available to educators today: norm-referenced measurements and criteria-referenced measurements. The most fundamental difference between these approaches is performance interpretation. Gronlund (1998, p. 26) describes the two assessment strategies as follows:

1. *Norm-referenced interpretation.* A relative ranking of a student among other students. (For example, he ranks as the third highest in a class of 35 students.)
2. *Criterion-referenced interpretation.* A description of the specific knowledge and skills each student can demonstrate. (For example, she can identify the parts of a microscope and demonstrate its use.)

(From *Assessment of Student Achievement,* 6th ed., by Norman E. Gronlund. Copyright © 1998 by Allyn & Bacon. Reprinted by permission.)

Norm-Referenced Tests

With a norm-referenced test, educators interpret a student's performance in relation to the norm group—the performances of students who have previously taken the examination. An example would be a student who scored in the 80th percentile on the SAT. This student's performance exceeded the performance of 80 percent of the students in the test's norm group.

Popham (1999) in his book *Classroom Assessment: What Teachers Need to Know* explains that norm-referenced interpretations are used to report students' results on academic aptitude tests such as the SAT, the Iowa Test of Basic Skills ITBS, the Metropolitan Achievement Tests (MAT), or the California Assessment Test (CAT). "Norm-referenced test interpretations are relative interpretations of students' performance because such interpretations focus on how a given student's performance stacks up in relation to the performance of other students" (p. 86).

Bracey (1998) explains that in nationally used tests, the most common norm is a national norm constructed by testing children all over the country. A norm-referenced test gives scores in relation to the norm, the 50th percentile. Test publishers determine the norm by trying out test questions to see if test items "behave properly." Proper behavior for most items means that 50 percent of the students get the item wrong. Some easier and some more difficult items will be used, but most will cluster in the 40 to 60 percent correct range. He says test creators want to make differential predictions that one cannot make if one creates test questions that everyone misses or everyone gets right. "It turns out that, if you choose items that, on average, 50 percent of the test takers get right and 50 percent get wrong, you end up with a test that distributes scores in a normal, bell-shaped curve and maximizes the dispersion of the scores" (p. 20). In order to ensure that the test items "behave properly" by causing 50 percent of the students to miss them, test makers must devise "distracters" or wrong answers presented in multiple choice questions to trick students into choosing a wrong answer. "Leaving aside whether trying to trick students into making mistakes is an appropriate activity for educators, let us note that this procedure can be a barrier to good test construction under some circumstances" (p. 20).

Test publishers determine the norm by trying out test questions to see if test items "behave properly."

Almost all nationally standardized tests are distributed by commercial testing firms, most of which are for-profit corporations. In order to construct the tests, publishers develop questions from the most common textbooks and curriculum materials. The sample questions are then rated by curriculum specialists to see if they have *content validity,* a term that means the item measures what it claims to measure. According to Bracey (1998), the questions are then tried on groups of people—or standardized—to see if, by means of statistical procedures, they "behave properly" so that about 50 percent of the test takers will answer the questions correctly for most questions.

Criterion-Referenced Tests

A criterion-referenced test scores performance in relation to a clearly specified set of behaviors. Once an assessment domain is defined, students' test performance can be interpreted according to the degree to which the domain has been mastered. Popham (1999) describes the difference between norm-referenced and criterion-referenced test interpretations as follows:

Standardized Tests

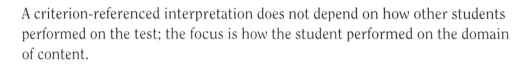

> . . . Instead of a norm-referenced interpretation such as the student "scored better than 85% of the students in the norm group," a criterion-referenced interpretation might be that the student "mastered 85% of the test's content and can be inferred to have mastered 85% of the assessment domain being represented by the test" (p. 99).

(From *Classroom Assessment: What Teachers Need to Know,* 2nd ed., by W. J. Popham. Copyright © 1999 by Allyn & Bacon. Reprinted by permission.)

A criterion-referenced test scores performance in relation to a clearly specified set of behaviors.

A criterion-referenced interpretation does not depend on how other students performed on the test; the focus is how the student performed on the domain of content.

One of the major problems with criterion-referenced tests is that testers have difficulty specifying educational outcomes with clarity. Another problem involves establishing a "cut-score" for passing or failing. Bracey (1998) comments that the idea of minimum competency tests was created to assure graduates had the minimal skills to graduate. However, this practice "reduced criterion-referenced tests to nothing more than norm-referenced tests without the norm" (p. 25). Another problem occurs when these tests are used for high-stakes decisions such as promotion, retention, or graduation eligibility. Since no test is perfectly accurate because of what test makers call "measurement error," Bracey is concerned that many states are currently implementing or planning to implement stiff sanctions against students, teachers, and administrators for not passing tests. He advocates taking the measurement error into account when setting cut-scores on high-stakes accountability tests.

Why Standardized Tests?

"Why have tests become so important? The short answer is that people lost confidence in their schools and the people who run them" (Bracey, 1998, p. 2).

Eisner (1994) agrees that many people have lost confidence in the capacity of schools to provide the quality education they believe they have paid for. The major source of their concern is often the decline of students' scores on the SAT. According to the College Entrance Examination Board (1989) from 1966 to 1990 the average SAT verbal score dropped 42 points (from 466 to 424) and the average SAT math score dropped 18 points (from 492 to 474). Eisner admits that the drop has been steady, yet the evidence is hardly adequate for evaluating the quality of American schools. "It takes only 6 missed items to account for a drop from 466 to 424 in the verbal section and only 4 missed items to explain a drop from 492 to 474 in the math section. My point here is not to provide an apology for dropping test scores, it is simply to provide an indication of the shallow analysis that has gone into the interpretation of the meaning of these scores" (1994, p. 3).

Eisner also wonders about the kind of predictive validity five or six multiple choice items have. (See examples on page 34.) He and many others speculate that perhaps the drop in the scores may be attributed at least in part to the diversity of the population taking the SATs. In the early years of the SAT, mostly white males trying to get into Ivy League colleges took the test. The SAT was introduced in 1926 as an efficient and economical instrument to help college admissions officers select the most promising students from among the increasing number of applicants (Schudson, 1972). Currently, many female and minority students with lower grade-point averages take the test because they want to attend college. Some educational theorists would contend that, rather than being alarmed at falling test scores, Americans should be encouraged that so many more students from diverse backgrounds are receiving opportunities for higher education.

Important to note is that Carl Campbell Brigham, the principal developer of the SAT, regarded the test "as merely a supplemental record" to the rest of the high school record. Furthermore, the American Educational Research Association, the American Psychological Association, and the National Council for Measurement in Education have published standards for test development and implementation which consider the use of test scores alone for decisions such as college admissions as "grave ethical violations" (Bracey, 1998, p. 11).

Important to note is that Carl Campbell Brigham, the principle developer of the SAT, regarded the test "as merely a supplemental record."

Wiggins (1989) feels that standardized testing evolved and proliferated because the school transcript became untrustworthy. "An 'A' in 'English' means only that some adult thought the student's work was excellent. Compared to what or whom? As determined by what criteria? In reference to what specific subject matter?" (p. 42).

The Increased Use of Standardized Tests

The increased use of standardized tests in the United States cannot be attributed to any one factor, but following are seven concerns or events that help to explain the growing emphasis on standardized tests in education over the last few decades.

Standardized tests are often viewed as the only solid measurement of school quality.

1. The launch of Sputnik in 1957 signaled the beginning of a curriculum overhaul to improve the mathematics and science curriculum so the United States could stay competitive in the space race against the USSR. Tests were widely used to measure improvement (Bracey, 1998).
2. Teachers inflated grades, giving high grades based upon subjective judgments (no criteria) and arbitrary selection of content (Wiggins, 1989).
3. Grades are ambiguous. An A or D sometimes includes variables such as attendance, behavior, neatness—not necessarily related to student achievement (O'Connor, 2002).
4. Publication of *A Nation at Risk* in 1983 created new anxieties about the "rising tide of mediocrity" in schools (Bracey, 1998).
5. SAT scores declined between 1966 to 1990 (College Entrance Examination Evaluation Board, 1989).
6. The Third International Mathematics and Science Study (TIMSS) press conference, attended by 300 people and reported in papers around the nation on November 20, 1996, released test results showing that American students were slightly above average in science and slightly below average in math (Bracey, 1998).
7. The public perceives large-scale assessments as the guardians of educational standards (Stiggins, 1994).

As Bracey (1998, p. 3) explains: "For those worried about the quality of the schools, the question became, 'If we can't trust people in schools to tell us about how well they are functioning, what can we trust?' In looking around for a means by which to evaluate schools, various outsiders discovered tests. Tests were external. Tests seemed objective. Best of all, tests in their multiple-choice formats were cheap. And once electronic scoring of answer sheets became a reality, the results could be known quickly."

Archbald and Newmann (1988) describe how newspapers rank schools according to scores and legislators are continually calling for uniform standardized testing programs. Standardized tests are often viewed as the only solid measurement of school quality. Despite the drawbacks of standardized testing, the fact remains that "standardized test scores allow simple comparisons between students, schools, districts, states, and nations. They are easily administrated, take little time away from instruction, and, with a long history of use by psychometricians and major institutions, they carry scientific credibility" (p. 52).

Guskey (2003) believes that large-scale assessments are used in most states today to rank-order schools and students for the purpose of accountability. But he says that "assessments designed for ranking are generally not good instruments for helping teachers improve their instruction or modify their approach to individual students" (p. 7).

Guskey and many others believe that teacher-made assessments that teachers administer on a regular basis are the assessments best suited to guide improvements in student learning.

> Guskey and many others believe that teacher-made assessments are best suited to guide improvements in student learning.

How Can Standardized Tests Be Used?

The debate over how standardized tests are being used and how they could be used in the future is ongoing. Bracey (1998, pp. 9–12) describes some of the possible uses and misuses of standardized tests:

Monitoring: Tests are sometimes used by teachers and parents as a "reality check" to determine if the test results correlate to other assessment indicators like classroom performance and report card grades. People have also begun to distrust grades because of grade inflation. Therefore, they tend to look to external instruments.

Diagnosis: Tests are used diagnostically to ascertain students' strengths and weaknesses. However, it is very difficult to use the typical commercial achievement test in a diagnostic fashion because there are too few items in any one skill area to give a reliable indication of any particular skill.

Teacher Accountability: Even though many districts and states are using standardized test scores to measure teacher accountability, it is a difficult concept to monitor. Two teachers may differ on how or what they teach. Eventually, all teachers will emphasize the material on the test if they will be held accountable. Problems also occur with assignment of teachers (best teachers have best classes) and external environment. Also, it is very difficult to use tests as accountability devices for teachers even after controlling for demographic variables.

Principal/Superintendent/Board Accountability: The same issue that applies to teachers applies to administrators. Some states are putting principals on probation for low test scores. It is possible to predict test score outcomes by comparing one school to other schools of similar demographic background by setting target goals. These programs are new, and it is too soon to evaluate their effectiveness.

Student Accountability (promotion, retention, and graduation decisions): Study after study has found retention in a grade does not work. A test score should never be used alone for making important decisions about students. Tests currently used for graduation eligibility are usually based on state curricula. Whether or not these tests are valid for other purposes needs to be evaluated in each instance.

Selection Decision: Tests are used to make discriminations among people to determine what type of educational experience they will have (college entry, gifted program, officer candidacy). "The hope has always been to match the experiences to people's needs and abilities, but it has not always worked out that way."

(Bracey, Gerald W. (1998) *Put to the Test: An Educator's and Consumer's Guide to Standardized Testing.* Bloomington, IN: Center for Professional Development and Services, Phi Delta Kappa International. Reprinted with permission.)

All the uses of standardized testing could become "abuses" if they are applied incorrectly.

How Can Standardized Tests Be Abused?

All the uses of standardized testing could become "abuses" if they are applied incorrectly. Students could be sorted and tracked in schools and not allowed the same opportunities for a quality education. Teachers and administrators could lose their jobs if students under their guidance don't perform well on tests, despite a wide variety of variables that could impact their performance. Teachers could sacrifice in-depth study of meaningful and creative learning experiences in exchange for "teaching for the tests." Students' individual needs and learning styles could be neglected in the movement to standardize curriculum, instruction, and assessments. In addition, teachers could decide not to accept the challenge of teaching students with behavior or learning problems because they might not get the $1,500 bonus for increasing students' scores on state tests. Everyone would want to teach the advanced students; no one would want to teach low-achieving or problem students. In addition, students could fail a grade or not graduate because of test scores despite the overwhelming research on the negative effects of retention (Darling-Hammond and Falk, 1997).

Amrein and Berliner (2003) are concerned about how the *No Child Left Behind Act of 2001* has made high-stakes testing more pervasive than ever before by mandating annual testing. Eighteen states currently use exams to grant or withhold diplomas, but the evidence shows that such tests actually decrease student motivation and increase the proportion of students who leave school early. Amrein and Beliner (2003) say that many researchers believe high-stakes testing is to blame for the higher dropout rate. Researchers found that dropout rates were 4 to 6 percent higher in schools with high school graduation exams. Another study by Jacob (2001) reported that students in the bottom quintile in states with high-stakes tests were 25 percent more likely to drop out of high school than were their peers in states without high-stakes tests. Sheldon and Biddle (1998, as cited in Amrein and Berliner, 2003) state, "Attaching stakes to tests apparently obstructs students' path to becoming lifelong, self-directed learners and alienates students from their own learning experiences in school" (p. 33).

Of course, everyone wants results and accountability, but how do educators ensure that every student has the same opportunity to learn? How do equity issues influence test scores? Discussion in the media and speeches by politicians and some business leaders make it sound like what happens in school is the only thing that has any impact on test scores. Noddings (1997) states that, since the educational status of parents is the single strongest predictor of how children will do in school, "It seems ludicrous to suppose that merely stating that 'all children will perform task T at level P' will actually accomplish much" (p. 184). Bracey (1998, pp. 12–13) warns that since a child only spends 9 percent of his or her life from birth to age eighteen in school, the public must take into consideration other factors influencing test scores:

- family income
- educational level of parents
- poverty
- motivation
- personal hygiene of students (sleep, food, etc.)
- cultural factors

Marzano (2003a) warns against schools or districts who rely on what he calls "indirect" learning data, often provided by the off-the-shelf standardized tests and even state-level standards tests. Such measures are indirect because they frequently do not adequately assess the content that is taught in the schools. "Direct data" includes tests that actually measure the content teachers teach in the school. It is more curriculum sensitive. Curriculum sensitive tests are clearly more dependent on the characteristics of schools and what teachers actually teach.

> Of course, everyone wants results and accountability, but how do educators ensure that every student has the same opportunity to learn?

Standardized Tests

Standardized tests do play a critical role in assessing students' abilities because of the validity and reliability of most of the tests. As several educational organizations have warned, however, to use test scores alone for making important decisions about students is a "grave ethical violation." Moreover, what happens if the standardized test is a poor test? A poorly designed test could affect the lives of students, parents, and educators for a lifetime.

The Need for Balanced Assessment

What happens if the standardized test is a poor test?

Stiggins (1994), like so many other educators, believes that classroom assessments provide data and feedback that standardized tests cannot. Classroom teachers guide students over time by using continuous observations to assess what is unique to an individual. Teachers provide constant feedback to students throughout their stages of development. Furthermore, teachers assess the growth and development of students and allow them to demonstrate their learnings addressing all eight of Gardner's multiple intelligences rather than focusing on verbal/linguistic and logical/mathematical—the intelligences emphasized on most standardized tests. The Venn diagram below illustrates some of the differences between standardized tests and classrooms assessments, along with one similarity.

Standardized Tests

Snapshot of Skills
one-time feedback
multiple-choice
standard questions
specific time limit
objective
no self-assessment
track students
emphasize reading and math skills
measure prior knowledge

Both methods are used to assess student achievement.

Classroom Assessments

Portfolio of Skills Development
continuous feedback
multiple formats
choice of questions
flexible time limits
objective/subjective
emphasis on self-assessment
track individual growth
emphasize multiple intelligences
measure application and transfer

Neither standardized tests alone nor teacher assessments alone can provide a true picture of a student's learning. Each by itself is insufficient. If educators are going to assess meaningful and authentic learning, they need to implement a balanced assessment program in order to make an informed and accurate evaluation of each student's achievement. The growing trend for state legislatures to mandate standardized tests at various grade levels and to administer school exit competency tests for graduation could be detrimental to students. These high-stakes tests should not be the determining factor for retention, promotion, or graduation, nor should they be used to distribute bonuses or pink slips. A standardized test is just one "snapshot" of a student's performance that needs to be combined with a variety of other assessment tools to provide a true portrait of the student as a learner. None of the assessment tools by themselves provide an accurate appraisal of a student's performance.

Standardized tests provide information only once a year. They reflect large-group increases or decreases in learning on an annual basis, and they can serve as gatekeepers for high-stakes decisions. But, Stiggins (2002) warns, "They cannot inform the moment-to-moment, day-to-day, and week-to-week instructional decisions faced by students and teachers seeking to manage the learning process as it unfolds" (p. 763).

In addition to the off-the-shelf standardized tests that do not necessarily align with the curriculum taught in the state, there are also state-level standards tests that are aligned to each state's standards. Although state tests based on state standards are a better option than off-the-shelf standardized tests, Marzano (2003b) feels that "they still don't live up to the challenge of providing a comprehensive and timely picture of student achievement. Neither a single test nor even a set of tests can ever address all the content that is taught within a given subject area at a given grade level" (p. 57).

The National Research Council (1999, cited in Marzano, 2003b, p. 57) concludes that standardized tests and state tests based on standards certainly have their place in K–12 education, but schools should not use them as a primary indicator of student learning.

A standardized test is just one "snapshot" of a student's performance.

Standardized Tests

PRIMARY

THIRD GRADE MATHEMATICS

How much of the figure is shaded?

- ○ 1/2
- ○ 3/8
- ● 1/4
- ○ 5/6

MIDDLE SCHOOL

EIGHTH GRADE MATHEMATICS

A swimming pool is 40 feet by 100 feet. What is the perimeter of the pool?

- A.   140 feet
- B.   180 feet
- Ⓒ   280 feet
- D.   400 feet
- E.   E. 600 feet

HIGH SCHOOL

ANTONYM

Clandestine

- A.   secretive
- B.   stoic
- Ⓒ   open
- D.   verbose
- E.   viscous

COLLEGE

ANALOGY

Procrastinate : delay :: prevaricate :

- A.   scold
- Ⓑ   lie
- C.   forge
- D.   incite

Thinking at Right Angles

Directions: In section A, list all the facts you know about standardized testing. In section B, list your feelings and associations. In section C, write a summary statement about standardized testing.

TOPIC: *Standardized Testing*

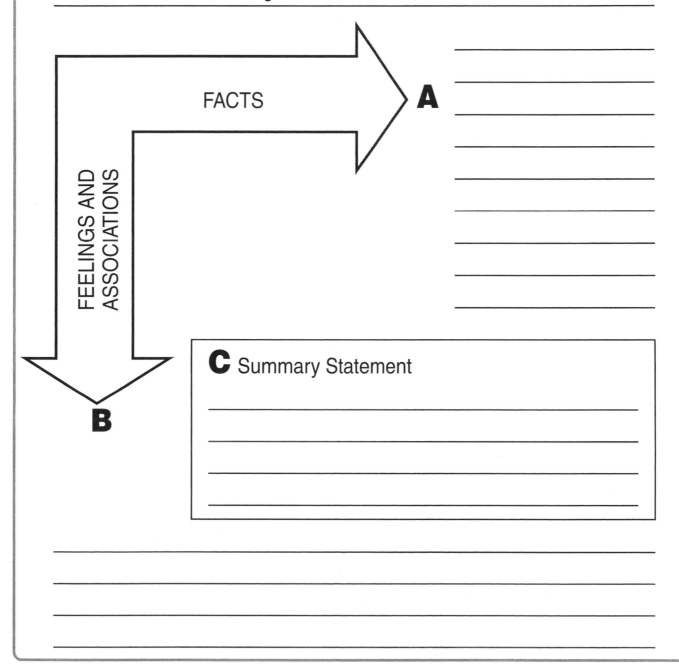

FACTS

A

FEELINGS AND
ASSOCIATIONS

B

C Summary Statement

Standardized Tests

1. Reflect on one standardized test you administered to your students. What do you remember about that test and the students' reactions to it?

_____

_____

_____

_____

2. Describe one of your own experiences when you took a standardized test.

_____

_____

_____

_____

3. How do you feel about the way standardized tests are used in your school district? Could you offer any suggestions to change how they are used?

_____

_____

_____

_____

MULTIPLE INTELLIGENCES

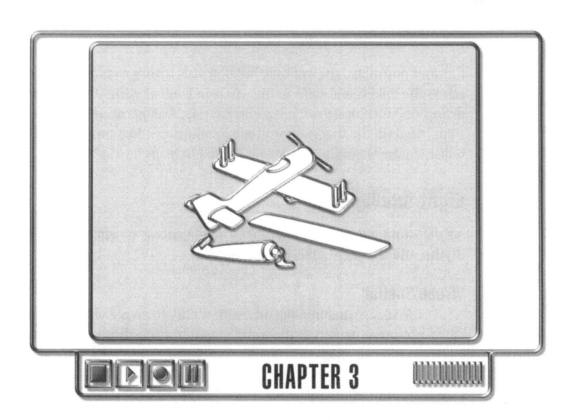

CHAPTER 3

"Multiple intelligences theory allows one
to assess the talents and skills of the whole
individual rather than just his or her verbal
and mathematical skill."
—FOGARTY AND STOEHR, 1995, P. 7

Multiple Intelligences

What Are Multiple Intelligences?

In his book *Frames of Mind,* published in 1983, Howard Gardner formulated a theory proposing an alternative to the traditional view of intelligence represented by IQ tests. Based upon his work with brain-damaged veterans at Boston's Veteran Medical Center and with children at Project Zero at Harvard's Graduate School of Education, he hypothesized that in addition to the verbal and mathematical intelligences that are traditionally recognized and fostered in schools, several other intelligences operate. Gardner theorized that human potential encompasses spatial, musical, and kinesthetic, as well as interpersonal and intrapersonal intelligences [adding the naturalist intelligence in 1995]. He further suggested that even though the eight intelligences are independent of one another, they do work together (Fogarty and Stoehr, 1995).

Gardner postulated the multiple intelligences theory would allow people to assess the talents and skills of the whole individual rather than the narrow definition of IQ measured in traditional tests. As Fogarty and Stoehr (1995) state, "Indeed, the theory of multiple intelligences does provide a more holistic natural profile of human potential than an IQ test" (p. 7).

Eight Intelligences

A brief summary of each of Gardner's intelligences, as explained by White, Blythe, and Gardner (1992, p. 128), follows:

Visual/Spatial

Visual/spatial intelligence is the ability to create visual/spatial representations of the world and to transfer those representations either mentally or concretely (architects, sculptors, engineers).

Logical/Mathematical

Logical/mathematical intelligence involves the ability to reason and to recognize abstract patterns (scientists, mathematicians).

Verbal/Linguistic

Verbal/linguistic intelligence involves ease in producing language (writers, poets, storytellers).

Gardner postulated that the multiple intelligences theory would allow people to assess the talents and skills of the whole individual.

Musical/Rhythmic

Musical/rhythmic intelligence includes sensitivity to pitch and rhythm (composers, instrumentalists).

Bodily/Kinesthetic

Bodily/kinesthetic intelligence involves using the body to solve problems, to create products, and to convey ideas and emotions (athletes, surgeons, dancers).

Interpersonal/Social

Interpersonal/social intelligence is the ability to understand other people and to work effectively with them (salespeople, teachers, politicians).

Intrapersonal/Introspective

Intrapersonal/introspective intelligence is personal knowledge about one's own emotions or self (writers, artists).

Naturalist (added by Gardner in 1995)

Naturalist intelligence is the ability to process and classify sensory input from nature such as flora and fauna (zoologists, environmentalists, conservationists).

Gardner's theory of multiple intelligences maintains that people possess several different capacities for creating products and solving problems.

Why Should We Use the Multiple Intelligences Approach?

Learning standards and district goals are important for all students to achieve, but educators need to honor the diversity of students and understand that not all students can achieve the standards at the same time and by only one mode of instruction or one method of assessment. Gardner's theory of multiple intelligences maintains that people possess several different capacities for creating products and solving problems. No one was more surprised than Gardner when the educational community embraced his theory. Teachers began to integrate a variety of learning experiences and assessments that addressed the eight intelligences.

Multiple Intelligences

GARDNER'S EIGHT INTELLIGENCES

Visual/Spatial
Images, graphics, drawings, sketches, maps, charts, doodles, pictures, spatial orientation, puzzles, designs, looks, appeal, mind's eye, imagination, visualization, dreams, nightmares, films, and videos

Logical/Mathematical
Reasoning, deductive and inductive logic, facts, data, information, spreadsheets, databases, sequencing, ranking, organizing, analyzing, proofs, conclusions, judging, evaluations, and assessments

Verbal/Linguistic
Words, wordsmith, speaking, writing, reading, papers, essays, poems, plays, narratives, lyrics, spelling, grammar, foreign languages, memos, bulletins, newsletters, newspapers, e-mail, faxes, speeches, talks, dialogues, and debates

Musical/Rhythmic
Music, rhythm, beat, melody, tunes, allegro, pacing, timbre, tenor, soprano, opera, baritone, symphony, choir, chorus, madrigals, rap, rock, rhythm and blues, jazz, classical, folk, ads and jingles

Bodily/Kinesthetic
Art, activity, action, experiential, hands-on experiments, try, do, perform, play, drama, sports, throw, toss, catch, jump, twist, twirl, assemble, disassemble, form, re-form, manipulate, touch, feel, immerse, and participate

Interpersonal/Social
Interact, communicate, converse, share, understand, empathize, sympathize, reach out, care, talk, whisper, laugh, cry, shudder, socialize, meet, greet, lead, follow, gangs, clubs, charisma, crowds, gatherings, and twosomes

Intrapersonal/Introspective
Self, solitude, meditate, think, create, brood, reflect, envision, journal, self-assess, set goals, plot, plan, dream, write, fiction, nonfiction, poetry, affirmations, lyrics, songs, screenplays, commentaries, introspection, and inspection

Naturalist
Nature, natural, environment, listen, watch, observe, classify, categorize, discern patterns, appreciate, hike, climb, fish, hunt, snorkel, dive, photograph, trees, leaves, animals, living things, flora, fauna, ecosystem, sky, grass, mountains, lakes, and rivers

From Fogarty, R., and Stoehr, J. (1995). *Integrating curricula with multiple intelligences: Teams, themes, and threads.* Arlington Heights, IL: IRI/SkyLight Training and Publishing. Reprinted with permission of LessonLab, Glenview, IL.

Sagor (2003) is concerned that in too many places, the implementation of standards-based education has led teachers to feel that they are supposed to "leave their creativity" at the door. He says often they are handed a canned, sometimes even scripted, curriculum. He also worries that in some locales, teachers are given a pacing chart that tells teachers not only *what* to teach but *when* to teach it. Creating a unit plan incorporating learning experiences and assessments using the multiple intelligences provides a creative way to teach the standards, differentiate instruction, and motivate students to learn in a variety of fun and challenging ways.

How Should We Use Multiple Intelligences?

Teachers are experimenting with a variety of instructional methods and assessments to evaluate students' achievement and progress toward meeting standards. Some educators are also experimenting with planning integrated instructional units that include learning experiences from all of the multiple intelligences. Using a graphic organizer such as the grid on page 51 to devise a unit plan helps groups of teachers focus on standards, integrate their curricula, brainstorm learning experiences and assessments, and decide on the key whole-class assessments to capture important concepts in the unit. This approach, as detailed below, helps teams of teachers or individual teachers plan a unit that synthesizes cooperative learning, higher-order thinking skills, portfolios, and performance tasks as well as rubrics with the multiple intelligences. (See page 45 for learning experiences and assessments classified by multiple intelligences.)

> Using the multiple intelligences provides a creative way to teach the standards, differentiate instruction, and motivate students.

Thirteen Steps to Develop a Unit Plan

The following format for developing a unit plan can be adapted to meet the needs of the teacher or a group of teachers:

1. Decide on a unit or theme that will last at least two to three weeks. The unit could be on a specific topic like oceanography or Greek mythology; a book, Stephen Crane's *The Red Badge of Courage;* or a country, Egypt. Some teachers choose to work on a thematic or integrated unit that connects several content areas. Some thematic units might include: health and wellness, justice in America, off to work we go, crime and punishment, a decade (the 1920s), the future, or heroes.
2. Draw a grid on large pieces of newsprint or use a blank grid.
3. Decide on the standards and/or benchmarks that will be the major goals of the unit. What should the students be able to do at the end of the unit?

Multiple Intelligences

4. Distribute sticky notes to each participant. Ask participants to brainstorm ideas for learning experiences or assessments for the unit and to write one idea per sticky note. Allow five minutes for individual thinking and writing. Remember to be specific—instead of writing "read a book about oceans," recommend *Chadwick the Crab*.

5. Read each idea and decide where it should go on the grid. Remember that many ideas cross over into other intelligences. For example, holding a mock trial to determine whether President Roosevelt suspected Pearl Harbor was going to be bombed could be classified as interpersonal, bodily/kinesthetic, or verbal/linguistic. Just place the idea where you think it goes or where you need more selections.

6. Review the grid to make sure there are five learning experiences or assessments for each intelligence. Remember, many activities are assessments. For example, creating a Venn diagram to compare and contrast Hemingway and Faulkner is an activity and it is also an assessment.

7. Decide on four learning experiences from the grid that would benefit the whole class. Consider the following criteria for selecting each experience:
   a. Does the experience help meet the standards?
   b. Does it include several intelligences? (Does it meet the needs of more students?)
   c. Is it worth the time to do it?
   d. Can it be assessed?
   e. Is it doable in my class? (Consider your time, resources, money, space, etc.)
   f. Is it fun and motivating?
   g. Will it meet the diverse needs of my students?

8. Write the four learning experiences in the boxes on the bottom of the grid. Remember that teachers on the team may select different whole-class experiences based upon their focus for the unit and the individual needs of their students.

9. Decide on how to assess the four learning experiences selected. Remember to combine traditional assessments (quizzes, tests, research reports) with performance assessments (logs, journals, portfolios, projects).

10. Create a culminating event to bring closure to the unit. The event should synthesize all the ideas and provide a showcase for the students to share their learnings with a wider audience. Examples of culminating events include mock trials, field trips, portfolio exhibitions, plays, costume days, a medieval banquet, a Renaissance fair, job fairs, and reenactments.

11. Develop a portfolio that includes three to four teacher-selected items to show students have met the standards. Allow students to select four or five other entries from the grid for their student choices.

12. Create rubrics to evaluate projects, group or individual performances, and the portfolio. Students can work in their groups to determine the criteria for each project. Teachers usually decide on four or five group projects and let students choose their groups. Groups could be divided as follows:
    a. research reports
    b. videotaped interviews
    c. simulations or performances
    d. newspaper stories
    e. PowerPoint™ presentations

Each group reviews samples of the product and determines the criteria that is necessary to create a successful product or performance. For example, the group creating the video could decide on three criteria regarding the sound element: loudness, dialogue clarity, and overall effect. They could then develop a rubric to help them prepare the video and to assess it for the final evaluation. The students and teacher may need to refine the rubric and add more focused descriptors as they work on the project, but at least creating the rubric makes the students aware of all the components they need to address. (See the Sample Rubric to Assess a Video Project below and the examples on pages 49–50.)

Sample Rubric to Assess a Video Project
VIDEO SOUND RUBRIC

Criteria/Scale	1	2	3	4
Loudness	Could not be heard	Difficult to hear	Could be heard most of the time	Could be heard all of the time
Dialogue Clarity	Dialogue could not be understood	Garbled	Erratic	Distinctive
Overall Effect	Detracts from video	Meets expectations	Supports the message of video	Enhances effect

13. Create a rubric to assess the portfolio. It could include criteria such as completeness, timeliness, understanding of content, visuals/graphics, reflections, mechanics, organization, etc. Many of the items included would have been graded previously; therefore, one grade using a weighted rubric could be used (see example on page 71). The students should be a part of the discussion about criteria and should self-evaluate their own portfolio using the rubric.

Multiple Intelligences

Using a Brain-Based Learning Approach

Students can become very involved in the planning of the multiple intelligences unit, thereby enriching their experiences while tapping their multiple intelligences. Some of them will want to write additional ideas for activities on sticky notes and add them to the grid. The choice that students have in determining what project or performance to work on and what items to select for their portfolios correlates with characteristics of an enriched environment that supports brain-based learning (Diamond and Hopson, 1998, pp. 107–108, as cited in Wolfe and Brandt, 1998). An enriched environment

The multiple intelligences unit plan enables teachers to make the most of students' individual differences.

- stimulates all the senses (but not necessarily all at once),
- has an atmosphere free of undue pressure and stress but is suffused with a degree of pleasurable intensity,
- presents a series of novel challenges that are neither too easy nor too difficult for the child at his or her stage of development,
- allows social interaction for a significant percentage of activities, and
- promotes the development of a broad range of skills and interests that are mental, physical, aesthetic, social, and emotional (Diamond and Hopson, 1998, as cited in Wolfe and Brandt, 1998, p. 11).

In addition to being a brain-based activity, the multiple intelligences unit plan enables teachers to make the most of students' individual differences and diversity, since students will gravitate toward their interests and strengths when they choose their projects and some of their portfolio entries. Many teachers feel comfortable developing a multiple intelligences unit with students because it fosters cooperative learning, integrated curriculum, interdisciplinary teaching, problem-based learning, performance tasks, authentic assessment, portfolios, higher-order thinking, and many other interactive strategies. Such an approach also taps the multiple intelligences of all students and promotes an enjoyable atmosphere of active learning.

The following chart classifies learning experiences and assessments by multiple intelligences. Three examples of unit plans organized by multiple intelligences and five examples of rubrics that can be used for assessment conclude the chapter. Opportunities to devise a unit plan using multiple intelligences and a rubric for a group project are also provided in the On Your Own section.

LEARNING EXPERIENCES

Verbal/Linguistic	**Logical/ Mathematical**	**Visual/Spatial**	**Bodily/ Kinesthetic**
Speeches Debates Storytelling Reports Crosswords Newspapers Internet	Puzzles Outlines Timelines Analogies Patterns Problem-solving Lab experiments Formulas	Artwork Photographs Math manipulatives Graphic organizers Posters, charts Illustrations Cartoons Props for plays Use of projector	Field trips Role playing Learning centers Labs Sports/games Cooperative learning Body language Experiments
Musical/Rhythmic	**Interpersonal**	**Intrapersonal**	**Naturalist**

Background music
Songs about books,
  people, countries,
  historic events
Raps
Jingles
Choirs
	Group video, film,
	  slides
	Team computer
	  programs
	Think-pair-share
	Cooperative tasks
	Jigsaws
	Conferences
		Reflective journals
		Learning logs
		Goal-setting journals
		Metacognitive
		  reflections
		Independent reading
		Silent reflection
		Diaries
			Outdoor education
			Environmental
			  studies
			Field trips (farm, zoo)
			Bird watching
			Nature walk
			Weather forecasting
			Stargazing
			Exploring nature
			Ecology studies
			Leaf identification

Teachers have been addressing the needs of their students by offering a repertoire of learning attributes and assessments. They vary the type of classroom activities and the projects and performances they assign. Using the multiple intelligences grid to plan a unit merely helps them to organize their learning experiences and make sure they engage in interactive teaching.

Multiple Intelligences

Oceanography Unit

Subject Area: _Integrated Unit—Elementary_   **Timeline:** _3–4 weeks_

Major Goals of Unit: _1. Knows the major differences between fresh and ocean waters._

2. Knows that an organism's patterns of behavior are related to the nature of that organism's environment.

3. Knows that the transfer of energy (e.g., through the consumption of food) is essential to all living organisms.

List at least three learning experiences or assessments under each intelligence.

Verbal/Linguistic	Logical/Mathematical	Visual/Spatial	Bodily/Kinesthetic
• _Read_ Chadwick the Crab. • _Read_ Curious Clownfish. • _Organize characters from_ Curious Clownfish _in chronological order._ • _Read_ Leroy the Lobster. • _Research the effects of oil slicks in the ocean and on marine life._	• _Measure with yarn the length of the blue whale._ • _Research sizes of whales._ • _Measure and draw sizes of whales in chalk on the blacktop._ • _Estimate the number of shells in container._ • _Classify the types of shells._	• _Create whale models to hang around the room._ • _Create a bulletin board about the ocean._ • _Create a mural of the ocean._ • _Make food chain mobiles._ • _Make a model of your favorite ocean creature._ • _Draw a web that shows attributes of sea creatures._	• _Play crab soccer._ • _Listen to ocean music and create a clay model of what you feel._ • _Imitate the movements of an octopus, crab, fish, or sea anemone._

Musical/Rhythmic	Interpersonal	Intrapersonal	Naturalist
• _Play ocean mood music (such as_ Free Willy _music)._ • _Listen to sounds of the ocean (whales, dolphins)._ • _Design instruments to mimic water sounds._	• _Choose an ocean animal to research and give an oral presentation with a partner._ • _In small groups, discuss products we receive from the ocean._ • _Interview students who have been to the ocean._ • _Do a KWL chart before you begin the unit._	• _Pretend you are an ocean animal._ • _Write a story about your life (or a day) as an animal that lives in the ocean._ • _Reflect on how pollution affects you._ • _Write a reflective journal on the sounds of the ocean._	• _Visit the aquarium._ • _Explore ocean-related careers._ • _Adopt an ocean animal._ • _Make predictions about ocean life._ • _Graph tides or water temperature._

1. Whole-class learning experiences:

Research report on an ocean animal	Oral presentation of report	Model of an ocean creature	Portfolio that contains 7 items

2. Whole-class assessments for learning experiences:

Checklist (point system)	Videotape for self-assessment	Criteria checklist	Rubric

3. Culminating event for unit:

Field trip to the local aquarium.

(Adapted from participants attending the Train the Trainers Authentic Assessment workshop, summer of 1996, Chicago, Illinois.)

Greek Mythology

Subject Area: _Integrated Unit—Middle School_   **Timeline:** _4–6 weeks_

Major Goals of Unit: 1. Communicate ideas in writing to describe, inform, persuade, and entertain.
2. Demonstrate comprehension of a broad range of reading materials related to Greek mythology.
3. Use reading, writing, listening, and speaking skills to research and apply information for specific purposes.

List at least three learning experiences or assessments under each intelligence.

Verbal/Linguistic 	**Logical/Mathematical** 	**Visual/Spatial** 	**Bodily/Kinesthetic**
• Read The Iliad. • Read The Odyssey. • Read Edith Hamilton's Mythology. • Write an original myth to explain a scientific mystery. • Write poems about mythology. • Write a eulogy for a fallen Greek or Trojan warrior.	• Use a Venn diagram to compare the Greeks and the Trojans. • Create original story problems that incorporate the Pythagorean theorem. • Draw a family tree of the twelve Olympians and their children. • Complete a timeline of Odysseus' trip home from Troy.	• Draw the battle plan for the Greeks' attack on Troy. • Draw Mt. Olympus. • Sketch the Greek gods and goddesses. • Create a video of the Olympic games. • Draw items that relate to mythology.	• Act out a Greek tragedy. • Re-create some of the Olympic events. • Act out a myth. • Create a dance for the forest nymphs. • Reenact the battle scene between Hector and Achilles.
Musical/Rhythmic 	**Interpersonal** 	**Intrapersonal** 	**Naturalist**
• Write a song for a lyre. • Pretend you are Apollo, God of Music, and CEO of Motown. • Select music that correlates with each god or goddess.	• Interview Helen about her role in the Trojan War. • Work in a group to create a computer crossword puzzle about mythology.	• Pretend you are a Greek soldier away from home for ten years. Keep a diary of your thoughts. • Write a journal about how you would feel if you were Prometheus chained to a rock. • Reflect on the effects of war on civilians.	• Using scientific data, predict how long it will take before anything grows after the Greeks destroy Troy and sow the fields with salt. • Describe the animals and plants on Mt. Olympus.

1. Whole-class learning experiences:	Read Hamilton's Mythology	Read excerpts from The Iliad and The Odyssey	Select a group project or performance	Portfolio that contains 7–10 items
	↕	↕	↕	↕
2. Whole-class assessments for learning experiences:	Teacher-made test	Write a paper comparing the Greeks to the Trojans.	Rubric to assess each one	Rubric created by class
3. Culminating event for unit:	Hold an exhibition in the school gym: where students and teachers dress up as favorite mythological characters. Invited guests view videos, portfolios, artifacts, and an original skit.			

Multiple Intelligences

EXAMPLES

The Red Badge of Courage Novel Unit

Subject Area: _American Literature—High School Social Studies_   **Timeline:** _3 weeks_

Major Goals of Unit: _1. Demonstrates competence in general skills and strategies for reading a variety of literary texts._

2. Demonstrates competence in the general skills and strategies of the writing process.

3. Understands major causes and effects of the Civil War.

List at least three learning experiences or assessments under each intelligence.

Verbal/Linguistic	Logical/Mathematical	Visual/Spatial	Bodily/Kinesthetic
• Read the novel The Red Badge of Courage by Stephen Crane. • Write a letter to President Lincoln about your feelings about the Civil War. • Interview a historian about the Battle of Chancellorsville.	• Graph the number of dead and wounded from major Civil War battles. • Compare the number of injured and dead in the Civil War to World War I, World War II, the Korean War, and the Vietnam War. • Create a Venn diagram comparing General Grant to General Lee.	• Draw a political cartoon about the Civil War. • Draw a mind map of the Civil War that contains major battles. • Draw a timeline of major events in the war. • Draw a book jacket for The Red Badge of Courage.	• Act out one key scene from The Red Badge of Courage. • Demonstrate marching drills used in the Civil War. • Visit a Civil War battleground, cemetery, or museum.

Musical/Rhythmic	Interpersonal	Intrapersonal	Naturalist
• Sing the songs the troops of the North and South sang while marching. • Learn the dances of the Civil War era. • Make up a ballad about Henry, the protagonist of The Red Badge of Courage.	• Read other books about buddies during war time, such as All Quiet on the Western Front, Catch 22, and For Whom the Bell Tolls. • Write and act out a dialogue between two military buddies in either Vietnam, Korea, or World War I or World War II.	• Keep a daily diary of boot camp. • Write a poem about your feelings. • Write a last will and testament in case you die in battle. • Write a eulogy for a soldier who died in battle.	• Find specific passages in The Red Badge of Courage. where author Stephen Crane tells about how war destroys nature. • Write how the environment (weather, rivers, terrain) impacts battle decisions. • Research the effects weapons of destruction have on the environment.

1. Whole-class learning experiences:	Read the novel The Red Badge of Courage	Create a mind map on Civil War battles	Select one group project or performance	Develop a portfolio that contains 7 items
2. Whole-class assessments for learning experiences:	Teacher-made test (numerical grade)	Checklist	Rubric to assess key criteria	Rubric to assess portfolio

3. Culminating event for unit:	Hold an exhibition where students display artifacts they selected from the grid to include in their personal portfolios. Invite guests to view videos, slides, and pictures from their projects.

Calling All Ecologists Rubric

WEIGHTED RUBRIC FOR AN INFOMERCIAL FOR AN ECOSYSTEM

4th Grade: *Science—Ecology*
Standards: *Give examples of habitats and niches in ecosystems.*
Explain how plants and animals interact and change their environments.

Scale: Criteria:	1 **Where is the remote control?**	2 **I am not hooked yet!**	3 **I am almost convinced.**	4 **You sold me!**	
Presentation Skills • Eye contact • Volume and tempo • Pronunciation • Enthusiasm	Keep practicing your script (1 out of 4)	On to the dress rehearsal (2 out of 4)	Cameras rolling (3 out of 4)	Ready for prime time (4 out of 4)	___x 6 = _____ 24
Content • Animal chosen • Habitat • Interaction • Problem • Solution	Back to the drawing board (1 out of 5)	On to the editing room (2 out of 5)	Ready for publishing (4 out of 5)	Best-seller (5 out of 5)	___x 7 = _____ 28
Visuals • Includes animal • Includes habitat • Colorful • Conveys a message of saving the environment	Under construction (1 out of 4)	Mom's fridge (2 out of 4)	Hallway display (3 out of 4)	Museum worthy (4 out of 4)	___x 8 = _____ 32
Organization • Hook • Presented in the allotted time (3–4 minutes) • Closure	You dropped your script (1 out of 4)	Pages out of order (2 out of 4)	Teleprompter is working (3 out of 4)	You are on your way to Hollywood (4 out of 4)	___x 4 = _____ 16

Student Comments:

Teacher Comments:

Total points = _____

Score
94–100 = A
86–93 = B
77–85 = C
Below 76 = Not Yet

Student: _____ **Teacher:** _____

Created by teachers on the assessment team of the Chattahoochee/Centennial/Northview Cluster in Fulton County, Georgia (2002). Used with permission.

Multiple Intelligences

PRIMARY

SIMULATION GAME RUBRIC

Criteria/ Scale	1	2	3	4
Clearly Stated Goal of Game	No goal	Vague goal	Goal stated, but difficult to reach	Clearly stated and attainable goal
Directions for Game	No directions	Directions are provided, but they are unclear	Clear directions provided	Clear and concise directions provided
Visuals for the Game	No visuals	Simple graphics provided	Clear diagram of game provided	Diagrams are clear and creative
Originality	Copied from another game	Ordinary idea	Ordinary idea with a different twist	Novel idea
Group Effort	Group members did not work well together	Members worked well some of the time	Members worked well most of the time	All members worked well together all the time

☐ Self-Assessment
☐ Group Assessment
☐ Teacher Assessment

Grading Scale
18–20 points = A
15–17 points = B
10–14 points = C
9 or below = Not Yet

Total Points _____
(20)

MIDDLE SCHOOL

GROUP WORK CHECKLIST

Self-assessment of my cooperative group skills for our team project.

1. I have participated in all tasks.   1   2   3   4   ☐
   • I performed my assigned role.
   • I helped team members.
   • I contributed to the group.

2. I have used time appropriately.   1   2   3   4   ☐
   • I stayed on task.
   • I monitored my team's activities.
   • I did not wait until the last minute to finish our project.

3. I behaved appropriately.   1   2   3   4   ☐
   • I was courteous to everyone.
   • I did not use put-downs.
   • I used appropriate language.

Scale
11–12 points = A
9–10 points = B
6–8 points = C
5 or below = Not Yet

Final Score _____
Final Grade _____

Student Comment:
_____
_____

Signed: _____ Date: _____

HIGH SCHOOL

PROBLEM-SOLVING RUBRIC

Criteria/ Scale	Novice	In Progress	Meets Expectations	Exceeds Expectations
Identifies Real Problem	Problem? What problem?	Someone else points out there is a problem.	Recognizes there is a problem.	Identifies real problem.
Gathers Facts	Does not realize the need to gather facts.	Able to gather one fact on own.	Knows where to look to obtain additional facts.	Accesses information to obtain all necessary facts.
Brainstorm Possible Solutions	Does not generate any solutions.	Generates one idea with someone's assistance.	Generates 2 or 3 solutions independently.	Generates 4 creative solutions independently.
Evaluates Effectiveness of Possible Solutions	Does not evaluate the effectiveness of possible solutions.	Recognizes pluses and minuses of some of the solutions.	Takes time to analyze effectiveness of each possible solution.	Uses reflection to decide what to do differently next time.

COLLEGE

RESUME RUBRIC

Assignment: Evaluate a resume in terms of five criteria.

Criteria/ Scale	No Chance 1	Try Again 2	Being Considered 3	Hired 4
Use of Correct Format • Address • Phone number • References	No form	Minimal form—three elements missing	Two elements of format missing	All elements of correct format included
Sequential Job History	No job history listed	Not in sequence	Listed in reverse order	Correct sequencing
Career Goals Clearly Stated	No goal stated	Needs more explanation	Goal adequately stated but needs polishing	Goal clearly stated
Overall Appearance • Margins • Spacing • Corrections	Three errors	Two errors	One error	No errors
Mechanics • Spelling • Grammar • Punctuation	Three or more errors	Two errors	One error	No errors

Scale   A = 18–20
B = 16–17
C = 13–15

Reprinted courtesy of Anita Zuckerberg, New York.

ON YOUR OWN

Unit Plan Using Multiple Intelligences Grid

Unit: _____ Grade Level: _____

Subject Area: _____ Timeline: _____

Major Goals of Unit: 1._____

　　　　　　　　　　　2._____

　　　　　　　　　　　3._____

List at least three learning experiences or assessments under each intelligence.

Verbal/Linguistic	Logical/Mathematical	Visual/Spatial	Bodily/Kinesthetic

Musical/Rhythmic	Interpersonal	Intrapersonal	Naturalist

1. Whole-class learning experiences:

2. Whole-class assessments for learning experiences:

3. Culminating event for unit:

Multiple Intelligences

Rubric Template for _____

Standard: _____

Criteria/Scale The Student:	1 Achieving Below the Standard	2 Approaching the Standard	3 Meeting the Standard	4 Exceeding the Standard	Score

From Burke, K.A., Fogarty, R., and Belgrad, S. (2002). *The Portfolio Connection: Student Work Linked to Standards*, 2nd ed., Arlington Heights, IL: SkyLight Professional Development. Reprinted with permission of LessonLab, Glenview, IL.

Multiple Intelligences

Review the thirteen steps to develop a unit plan using the multiple intelligences.
Complete the following stem questions:

1. One thing I learned about the multiple intelligences theory was . . .

2. One thing I want to try is _____
   because . . .

3. I feel my students would benefit from my incorporating multiple intelligences into my
   teaching because . . .

4. I feel I can differentiate my teaching to meet the needs of my students because . . .

PORTFOLIOS

CHAPTER 4

"A portfolio is more than just a container full of
stuff. It's a systematic and organized collection
of evidence used by the teacher and student
to monitor growth of the student's knowledge,
skills, and attitudes in a specific subject area."

—VAVRUS, 1990, P. 48

What Is a Portfolio?

"A portfolio is a collection of student work gathered for a particular purpose that exhibits to the student and others the student's efforts, progress or achievement in one or more areas." This working definition of portfolios was developed at the Northwest Regional Educational Laboratory in Portland, Oregon (cited in Johnson and Rose, 1997, p. 6). Carr & Harris (2001) define portfolio as a "purposeful, integrated collection of student work showing effort, progress, or achievement in one or more areas. Usefulness for instruction and assessment is enhanced when students select the items for their portfolios, self-reflection is encouraged, and criteria for success are clear" (p. 181).

A portfolio has a

purpose and a focus.

A portfolio is more than just a collection of stuff randomly organized and stuck in a folder. A portfolio has a *purpose* and a *focus*. The organization and the contents of portfolios differ according to the purpose and the type of the portfolio.

A portfolio may contain:

1. *Creative cover*—to depict the topic
2. *Letter to the reader*—to explain the cover and to welcome the readers
3. *Table of contents*—to display organization
4. *Six or seven student artifacts*—to showcase work selected by teachers and students
5. *Reflections*—to reveal student insight
6. *Self-evaluation*—to analyze strengths and weaknesses
7. *Goal-setting page*—to set new short-term and long-term goals
8. *Conference questions (optional)*—to provide the audience with key questions

Additional items that could be included in a portfolio are

- reflections or comments from peers about the artifacts;
- comments from parents or significant others;
- descriptions of major concepts learned; and
- a bibliography of sources used.

Purpose of the Portfolio

The first step in creating a portfolio is to determine the purpose of the portfolio. The contents need to be aligned to the purpose or rationale for implementing portfolios. A portfolio can be used to

1. document meeting district, state, or national standards;
2. connect several subject areas to provide an integrated assessment of the student;
3. chronicle a student's growth and development over extended periods of a semester, year, or clusters of grades (K–2, 3–5, 7–9, 10–12);
4. document the key concepts taught by teachers; and
5. share at a job interview, promotion, or college entrance review.

The purpose of the portfolio will determine the type of portfolio and the process to be used in developing the portfolio. It is not unusual for a portfolio to combine several purposes to meet the needs of the students or school.

In addition, portfolios motivate students to learn. Portfolios help some students achieve self-actualization experiences identified by Abraham Maslow (1971) as the need for a sense of personal fulfillment. Csikszentmihalyi (1990, as cited in Marzano, 2003b, p. 148) has identified four factors critical to successful completion of self-actualizing experiences that he refers to as "flow experiences":

1. the freedom to set clear goals that are highly meaningful to the individual,
2. having the resources to carry out the goals and becoming immersed in the act of trying to accomplish them,
3. paying attention to what is happening and making changes when necessary, and
4. enjoying immediate short-term successes while keeping an eye on the ultimate goal.

Portfolios help all students achieve their own sense of flow.

A portfolio can be used to chronicle a student's growth and development.

Types of Portfolios

Once the primary purpose for creating a portfolio has been determined, educators must select the type of portfolio that would best fulfill the purpose. These types may also be combined to correlate with the purpose for creating the portfolio. Review the list of portfolio types on the next page.

TYPES OF PORTFOLIOS

1. Writing—dated writing samples to show process and product
2. Process Folios—first and second drafts of assignments along with the final product to show growth
3. Literacy—combination of reading, writing, speaking, and listening pieces
4. Best Work—student and teacher selections of the student's best work
5. Unit—one unit of study (e.g., Egypt, angles, frogs, elections)
6. Integrated—a thematic study that brings in different disciplines (e.g., "health and wellness"—language arts, science, math, health, and physical education)
7. Yearlong—key artifacts from an entire year to show growth and development
8. Career—important artifacts (resumés, recommendations, commendations) collected for showcase employability
9. Standards—evidence to document meeting standards

The portfolio helps the classroom environment become a seamless web of instruction and assessment.

Hansen (1992) advocates using self-created literacy portfolios by asking students to include what they are like outside the classroom. Students can include pictures of relatives, awards or ribbons they have won in athletic events, lists of books or magazines about rock stars, sports, hobbies, or anything that interests them. The key to the portfolio is the discussion the items generate. Every adult and student involved in a literacy portfolio project creates a literacy portfolio. "Whether or not we know ourselves better than anyone else does, our portfolios give us the opportunity to get to know ourselves better" (Hansen, 1992, p. 66).

Krogness (1991) suggests that students list their goals at the beginning of each year. This goal setting allows them to learn what they value and focus their attention on meeting their goals.

Why Should We Use Portfolios?

The portfolio helps the classroom environment become a seamless web of instruction and assessment. "If carefully assembled, portfolios become an intersection of instruction and assessment; they are not just instruction or just assessment, but, rather, both. Together, instruction and assessment give more than either give separately" (Paulson, Paulson, and Meyer, 1991, p. 61).

Wolf (1989), Vavrus (1990), Paulson et al. (1991), Lazear (2003), and many others recommend portfolios because they can be used as the following:

- tools for discussion with peers, teachers, and parents
- demonstrations of students' skills and understanding

- opportunities for students to reflect on their work metacognitively
- chances to examine current goals and set new ones
- documentation of students' development and growth in abilities, attitudes, and expressions
- demonstrations of different learning styles, multiple intelligences, and cultural diversity
- options for students to make critical choices about what they select for their portfolio
- evidence that traces the development of students' learning
- connections between prior knowledge and new learning

Searfoss (cited in Glazer and Brown, 1993) also talks about the importance of blending instruction and assessment. The final product is important, but the process is equally important and probably conveys more about how the student learns. "Assessing process means we cannot act alone; we need our students involved in observing and monitoring their own products. By helping students focus on process, we guide them to discover for themselves how they can continually improve a product as they create it. Students learn how to 'fit things' as they arise, rather than waiting until the teacher identifies them as 'incorrect' or 'unclear'" (p. 16). The process of metacognition—thinking about one's thinking—helps students become more self-reflective and more empowered as stakeholders in their own learning.

The final product is important, but the process is equally important.

Metacognition ⟶ **Reflective Entry**
(inner dialogue)   (written description)

How Can We Implement Portfolios?

Educators have developed a variety of creative and intricate portfolio systems, but for teachers just embarking on the portfolio journey, it might be best to start simply. The portfolio process in its simplest form includes three basic steps, as shown below.

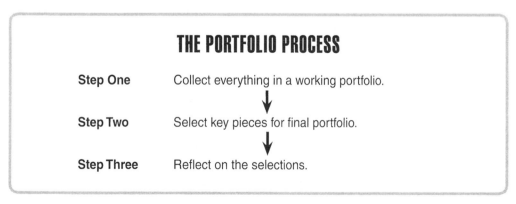

THE PORTFOLIO PROCESS

Step One	Collect everything in a working portfolio.
Step Two	Select key pieces for final portfolio.
Step Three	Reflect on the selections.

Portfolios

Collect

Educators, in most cases, recognize the benefits of using portfolios to show the growth and development of their students. Unfortunately, they also recognize the tremendous organizational problems and increased time commitment associated with implementing a portfolio system.

Working Portfolios

To simplify the implementation of the system, note the first step in the collection process is to develop a working portfolio. The working portfolio is where students store all the items they have collected before they make their selections for the final, or showcase, portfolio. Various methods for storing items include:

- large cardboard boxes
- cereal boxes
- file folders
- accordion files
- computer disks
- videos or CD-ROMs
- file cabinets

Creating a working portfolio is similar to traditional assessment because students usually collect their work. Work should still be sent home and brought back. Teachers may choose to make a copy of very important assignments before they are sent home, just in case of loss or damage. Even if students lose some of their work, there should still be enough work left from which to choose for the final portfolio. This first step is not much different than a teacher asking students to keep a folder or a notebook of their work.

Variety of Artifacts

One of the characteristics of working portfolios that sets them apart from more traditional writing folders, however, is that they should contain a variety of work that reflects different modalities. Students should have more than just worksheets or homework assignments in their working portfolio; they should collect artifacts including cassette tapes, videotapes, pictures, projects, performances, rough drafts, journals, logs, artwork, musical work, computer disks, and assignments that feature work from all the multiple intelligences. If the portfolio is to be a true portrait of the student as a learner, it needs to be richly textured and comprehensive. It also must assess more than just one of the multiple intelligences—in this case, usually the verbal/linguistic intelligence. A writing folder is a writing folder. A portfolio is much more.

Select

After most of the quarter or semester is spent collecting items, the selection process usually involves three major questions:

1. Who should select the items that go into the final portfolio?
2. What items should be selected?
3. When should these items be selected?

Who Should Select Items?

In most cases, both teachers and students select the items to be included in the final portfolio. The teacher needs to show evidence that the students met school goals or standards and that they understand the basic concepts of the course. If students were allowed to choose all the items, they would probably select their best or favorite work, but those items wouldn't necessarily provide a balanced analysis that documents learning. After the teacher has selected some general items, then students should have the freedom to choose items that they want to include to showcase their strengths and talents.

The first step is to develop a working portfolio.

In addition, parents and peers sometimes select items for the portfolio and write a comment or reflection about the piece or pieces. The selection process varies, however, depending on the purpose and type of the portfolio. If the purpose of the portfolio were to meet district standards, then the teacher would have to request pieces that provide evidence of meeting those standards. Sometimes the selection could involve both the teacher and the student. For instance, the teacher may require a narrative writing piece to meet standards, but the student can choose which one of his or her narrative pieces to include. The teacher sets the parameters, but the student has some choice within those parameters.

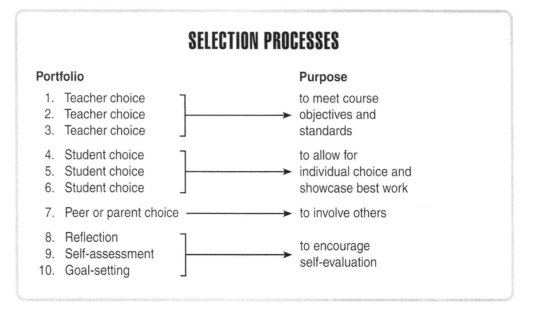

SELECTION PROCESSES

Portfolio		Purpose
1. Teacher choice	⎤	to meet course
2. Teacher choice	⎬ →	objectives and
3. Teacher choice	⎦	standards
4. Student choice	⎤	to allow for
5. Student choice	⎬ →	individual choice and
6. Student choice	⎦	showcase best work
7. Peer or parent choice	→	to involve others
8. Reflection	⎤	to encourage
9. Self-assessment	⎬ →	self-evaluation
10. Goal-setting	⎦	

The motto educators need to adopt is "less is more."

Regardless of who selects the entries, Rolheiser, Bower, and Stevahn (2000) believe that interested parties need to respond to students' entries. They believe the feedback should generate positive energy and motivation for continued learning. They also suggest that the responders ask students "what they think, what helped them, and how they dealt with challenges" (p. 65).

What Items Should Be Selected?

The motto that educators need to adopt for the selection process if they are going to maintain their sanity and make this process manageable is "less is more." It is not necessary to include all of the artifacts in the final portfolio. Even though some students think all of their work is wonderful and they just can't eliminate anything, the very process of reviewing their work and deciding what is appropriate is metacognitive. Most portfolios contain seven to twelve items. Teachers should not have to bring a wagon to school to haul home portfolios. Keep it simple. Fewer items provide more opportunities for in-depth discussion and more targeted feedback and analysis.

Many teachers like to include selection criteria such as "select a piece that is your most unsatisfying piece and discuss why" or "select the piece you would like to do over and tell why" or "select the piece that you just don't understand and explain why." These criteria provide insightful information about the learner and his or her learning process. By viewing the not-so-best work, the audience gets a truer picture of the student's strengths and weaknesses and why he or she set goals for improvement. If students only select their best work for all portfolios, the students may increase their self-esteem, but

LESS IS MORE

Mrs. Bateman has had some problems with the "selection" phase of her portfolio process.

The evidence in the final portfolio needs to reflect both strengths and weaknesses.

the students, teachers, and parents may develop a distorted or rose-colored opinion of the student's abilities. The "best work" portfolio sometimes appears "fluffy" and portrays a portfolio as a "scrapbook of stuff" rather than a collection of evidence that the student met learning standards, district goals, or course objectives. The portfolio must also include rigorous assessments that document a student's ability and help teachers modify their instruction or adapt the curriculum to meet the student's needs. The evidence in the final portfolio needs to reflect both strengths and weaknesses and correlate to traditional assessments such as teacher-made tests and standardized tests. The portfolio grade will probably be higher than traditional test grades because students have more time to revise and perfect their work.

When Should Items Be Selected?

"A timeline for data gathering is essential. For some components of the portfolio, the timeline will indicate critical points in the academic year: beginning, middle, and end of year. For other components, a schedule of regular data gathering may be daily, weekly, and monthly." (Shaklee, Barbour, Ambrose, and Hansford, 1997, p. 51).

Portfolios

The timing for selecting items for the final portfolio depends once again on the purpose and type of portfolio. Many teachers find it more manageable to have the students complete unit portfolios throughout the year. Once the unit is complete, the teacher saves the portfolio contents and returns the notebook or permanent final portfolio container to the students for their next unit portfolio. At the end of the year, the teacher distributes the four or five unit portfolios and asks students to select items for their final yearlong portfolio. The students then choose about ten to twelve items based upon selection criteria such as the following:

1. Select one item from the beginning of the year and a similar item from the end of the year and comment on your growth.
2. Select your favorite artifact and explain why.
3. Select your least favorite artifact and explain why.
4. Select an artifact that will surprise people and explain why.

TIMELINE SCENARIOS

Unit Portfolio

1. Collect items for three or four weeks.
2. Select and reflect on items two weeks prior to the end of the unit.
3. Conduct conferences in the last week.
4. Grade portfolio the last week.

Semester Portfolio

1. Collect items the entire semester.
2. Select seven to ten final items for the portfolio four weeks before the end of the semester.
3. Allow one week for students to select, reflect, and organize the portfolios.
4. Allow one week for conferences.
5. Allow one week for grading.

Yearlong Portfolio

1. Collect one to two items each week.
2. Review all items at the end of each quarter and select three or four items. Date all items.
3. Repeat process each quarter. Students write reflections on each item.
4. Four weeks before the end of school, select the final ten to twelve items for the portfolio.
5. Allow two to three weeks for reflection, organization, and conferencing.
6. Allow one to two weeks for grading.

Reflect

"Most of the best research on cognitive development suggests that it is extremely important to create situations in which students must think about their own thinking, reflect on the ways in which they learn and why they fail to learn. It's clear that the more students are aware of their own learning processes, the more likely they are to establish goals for their education and the more deeply engaged they are in those processes" (Mills-Courts and Amiran, as cited in Belanoff and Dickson, 1991, p. 103). Portfolios enable teachers and students to create "spaces" for students to reflect on their progress. Martin-Kniep (2000) says, "Such reflection could be a letter to the reader, an introduction to the portfolio, or reflective statements that accompany the various portfolio entries or artifacts. A portfolio without a student's reflection is not really a portfolio, but rather a collection of work that is hard to decipher without commentary from its author" (p. 67).

Labeling

The first and easiest step in the reflection process involves asking students to attach a label to each artifact in the portfolio. The labels could include:

- "best work"
- "most difficult"
- "most creative"
- "a nightmare"
- "first draft—more to come"

Reflection is the heart and soul of the portfolio.

Another strategy to introduce students to the reflection process is to have them write their reflections, reactions, or descriptions on sticky notes and then attach the sticky notes to each item. Sometimes they may rewrite these initial reflections when they select the piece for their final portfolio. Other times, they'll just edit them slightly. Occasionally, they'll include their initial reflection from when they completed an item and then add another reflection (upon further reflection) to provide insight after more time has elapsed.

Stem Questions

Some students become adept at writing descriptions and reflections of their work without any prompts. Many students, however, stare at their portfolio pieces and have no idea what to write. Teachers can prime the pump by either assigning a stem question or allowing students to select a stem to complete.

Portfolios

REFLECTIVE STEMS

1. This piece shows I've met standard #_____ because . . .
2. This piece shows I really understand the content because . . .
3. This piece showcases my _____ intelligence because . . .
4. If I could show this piece to anyone—living or dead—I would show it to _____ because . . .
5. People who knew me last year would never believe this piece because . . .
6. This piece was my greatest challenge because . . .
7. My (parents, friend, teacher) liked this piece because . . .
8. One thing I have learned about myself is . . .

Goal Setting

Goal setting is a part of reflection. Students need to set goals within a predetermined period of time. Goals are like road maps because they guide the student's journey. Pete and Fogarty (2003) say goals "provide the inspiration to begin the journey and the motivation to keep going" (p. 73). Students can set both short- and long-term goals in their portfolios.

At each portfolio conference, the student can reflect on his or her progress and set new goals. Since the standards movement sometimes dictates the end result or outcome, students should set robust and rigorous intermediate or final goals and try to not only meet them, but exceed them.

Mirror Page

Another method to help students gain insight into their work is to ask them to organize their portfolio so that they place the item or piece of evidence on one page and write a description of the piece, followed by a reflection or reaction to it, on the facing page. The proximity of the reflection to the piece of evidence helps the portfolio creator as well as the reader focus on examining the piece more carefully by referring to the elements being described.

Piece of student work	Description of work
	Reflection on work

The description requires the student to explain the piece of work and share his or her understanding of its importance. Also, the description provides the teacher with a more in-depth analysis of student learning. The description could be elaborated upon during the conference, but the written description helps to clarify whether or not the student understands the basic concept of the assignment. The reflection, on the other hand, helps the student understand how he or she feels about the piece by asking himself or herself questions such as:

1. What does this piece show about me?
2. What did I do well in this piece?
3. What do I still need to practice?
4. What help do I need?

Student Reflection

A seventh-grade student was asked to include in his portfolio his most difficult math assignment and write why it was his most difficult piece. He included an assignment on word problems and wrote the following piece, entitled "My Most Difficult Work":

> If I had to choose one, I would choose the word problems that we did. I found them the most difficult out of the things that we did. I found them the most difficult because I had to think about them for a while before I could get an answer especially since I work at a slow pace. We didn't have enough time for me to be able to take my time and think them over. I was able to find the answer most of the time but other kids work at a faster rate than I do so they were able to get more of the answers. I was glad we got to work in groups because it showed me that I was not the only kid who was having trouble with them. I think that it also helped me because some people could understand parts of the problem better than others and we could also learn how they found out the answers which will help us out in the future. I am going to try to correct it by getting a book on word problems and tips on how to solve them. I am also going to be an engineer so I will need to get good at them and take classes that deal with them when I get older.

The teacher was amazed when she read the reflection because she had always thought mathematics came very easily to the student. She said she gained new insight into the student as a learner and a person by reading his reflection. Her comment was, "I ask you, does this child understand the content, the process, and himself?" (personal correspondence, 1996).

The description provides the teacher with a more in-depth analysis of student learning.

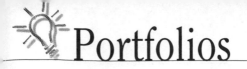

Portfolios

A portfolio without reflection is really just a notebook of stuff!

A portfolio without reflections is really just a notebook of stuff! The power of the portfolio is derived from the descriptions, reactions, processing pieces, and metacognitive reflections that help students achieve their goals. Conducting teacher-student conferences and peer conferences to discuss the portfolios helps synthesize the learning and celebrate the successes. This chapter has just addressed the tip of the iceberg about portfolios, but the three basic steps remain the key: collect, select, reflect. For educators and students just beginning the portfolio process, start small! Once the first portfolios are produced, the process can be altered, extended, and elaborated upon to meet the needs of the teacher, the school, and, most importantly, the student.

EXAMPLES

PRIMARY

LANGUAGE ARTS PORTFOLIO

Integrated Unit on Spiders

Table of Contents

1. Letter to parents about what students have learned
2. Book review of *Charlotte's Web*
3. Web of characteristics of spiders
4. Watercolor picture of spiders
5. Tape of student reading story about spiders
6. Original short story (first and final drafts) about a spider
7. Science report on arachnids
8. Spider rap song
9. Pictures of group project on spiders
10. Self-assessment using a criteria checklist

MIDDLE SCHOOL

GEOMETRY PORTFOLIO

Table of Contents

1. My Math Photos Journal
2. Two geometry tests—corrections included
3. Glossary of geometry terms
4. Drawings of geometric shapes
5. Three problem-solving logs
6. String geometric design
7. Video of group project on angles
8. Essay on video, *Why Math?*
9. Research on math-related careers
10. Self-evaluation of portfolio using rubrics
11. Goal setting for next quarter

HIGH SCHOOL

BIOLOGY PORTFOLIO

Table of Contents

1. Reports on careers related to the field of biology
2. One lab report
3. One problem-solving log
4. Pamphlet on diabetes (group project)
5. Video of group presentation on the circulatory system
6. Essay on germ warfare
7. Research paper on AIDS
8. Tape-recorded interview with college biology professor about AIDS
9. Self-evaluation of portfolio using rubric
10. Goal-setting web

COLLEGE

AMERICAN HISTORY PORTFOLIO

Table of Contents

1. Annotated bibliographies of five books written about the Civil War
2. Reading list of fifty books and articles related to the Civil War
3. One abstract of a research article
4. Tape of interview with local historian
5. Journal entries of trip to Gettysburg
6. Map of the Battle of Gettysburg
7. Video of oral presentation on Pickett's charge
8. Research paper on military tactics used at the Battle of Gettysburg
9. Venn diagram preparing Battle of Gettysburg and Battle of Chancellorsville
10. Critique of TV miniseries *The Civil War*
11. Peer evaluation of portfolio using rubric

Portfolios

Portfolio Checklist

Standard: Use reading, writing, listening, and speaking skills to research and apply information for specific purposes.

Clustered Criteria Checklist

Criteria/Performance Indicators	Not Yet 0	Some Evidence 1
Form		
• Spelling		
• Grammar		
• Sentence structure		
Visual Appeal		
• Cover		
• Artwork		
• Graphics		
Organization		
• Completeness		
• Timeliness		
• Table of contents		
Knowledge of Key Concepts		
• Key concepts		
• Evidence of understanding		
• Application		
Reflections		
• One per piece		
• Depth of reflection		
• Ability to self-assess		

Student Comment:

Scale
13–15 = A
11–12 = B
9–10 = C

Weighted Rubric for Portfolio

(Developed from Checklist)

Student: _____ Subject: _____ Date: _____

Standard: Use reading, writing, listening, and speaking skills to research and apply information for specific purposes.

Criteria	Indicators	Does Not Meet Standards 1	Approaching the Standards 2	Meets State Standards 3	Exceeds State Standards 4	Score
Form	• Spelling • Grammar • Sentence structure	2–3 errors	1–2 errors	0 errors	0 errors and a high level of writing	__ x 3 __ (12)
Visual Appeal	• Cover • Artwork • Graphics	Missing 2 elements	Missing 1 element	All 3 elements included	All 3 elements are creatively and visually appealing	__ x 4 __ (16)
Organization	• Completeness • Timeliness • Table of contents	Missing 2 elements	Missing 1 element	All 3 elements included	All 3 elements demonstrate high level of organization	__ x 5 __ (20)
Knowledge of Key Concepts	• Key concepts • Evidence of understanding • Application	Evidence of key concepts included in portfolio	Evidence of basic level of understanding of key concepts	Evidence of high level of understanding of key concepts	Evidence of ability to apply knowledge to new situations	__ x 6 __ (24)
Reflections	• One per piece • Depth of reflection • Ability to self-assess	Missing 2 or more reflections	Missing 1 reflection	Insightful reflections for each piece	Reflections show insightfulness and ability to self-assess	__ x 7 __ (28)

Student Comment:

Teacher Comment:

Scale
A = _____
B = _____
C = _____
D = _____

Final Score: _____
(100)

Final Grade: _____

EXAMPLES

Reconstruction Portfolio
Portfolio Checklist

5th Grade: Social Studies–Reconstruction

Standards:
- Cause and effect
- Analysis of the impact on environment and settlement patterns
- Physical maps to draw conclusions
- Identification of key events in Reconstruction with emphasis on economic and philosophical differences between the North and South

Assignment: Create a portfolio containing the assignments required.

Criteria/Performance Indicators	Not Yet 0	Yes 1
Cover: Do you have . . .		
• Your name		
• Title		
• Picture		
• Date		
Content: Do you have . . .		
• A newspaper article		
• A poster of the 13th, 14th, and 15th amendments		
• Diary entry		
• First free choice		
• Second free choice		
• Reflection for each piece		
Organization: Do you have in this order . . .		
• Cover		
• Table of contents		
• Newspaper article		
• Reflection on newspaper article		
• Poster		
• Reflection on poster		
• Diary entry		
• Reflection on diary entry		
• First free choice		
• Reflection on first free choice		
• Second free choice		
• Reflection on second free choice		
Mechanics: Did you check for accuracy of . . .		
• Capitalization		
• Punctuation		
• Spelling		
• Grammar		
Visual Appeal:		
• Is your work neat and visually attractive?		
• Is your work in a folder?		

Student Comment:

Scale
25–28 = A
21–24 = B
17–20 = C
Not Yet

Total Points: _____

Created by teachers on the assessment team of the Chattahoochee/Centennial Northview Cluster in Fulton County, Georgia (2002). Used with permission.

ON YOUR OWN

Portfolio Planner

Purpose of portfolio: _____

_____

Type: _____   Standards addressed: _____

Timeline: _____   _____

Working Portfolio Process	**Final Portfolio Process**

Items to collect:

_____

_____

_____

Three stem questions for reflections:

1. _____

2. _____

3. _____

Portfolios

Portfolios

Review this PMI graphic organizer (de Bono, 1992) and write your own ideas about the pluses, minuses, and interesting aspects of portfolios.

Use of Portfolios
Pluses
Minuses
Interesting Aspects

PERFORMANCE TASKS AND RUBRICS

CHAPTER 5

"Performance assessment typically requires students to respond to a small number of more significant tasks rather than respond to a large number of less significant tasks."

—POPHAM, 1999, P. 161

Performance Tasks and Rubrics

What Are Performance Tasks?

Teachers motivate students to learn when they create curriculum units that address the standards, ask essential questions, and establish clear learning goals. Marzano, Marzano, and Pickering (2003) state that teachers exhibit an assertive level of classroom control by

- "establishing learning goals at the beginning of a unit of instruction,
- providing feedback on the goals,
- continually and systemically revisiting the goals, and
- providing summative feedback regarding the goals" (p. 50).

Performance tasks encompass many skills and usually have a direct application to real tasks.

Performance tasks embed the standards and are more than activities that teachers assign students. They encompass many skills and usually have a direct application to real tasks people are asked to do in everyday life. Lewin and Shoemaker (1998, p. 5) feel that a performance task has the following key characteristics:

1. Students have some choice in selecting the task.
2. The task requires both the elaboration of core knowledge content and the use of specific processes.
3. The task has an explicit scoring system.
4. The task is designed for an audience larger than the teacher; that is, others outside the classroom would find value in the work.
5. The task is carefully crafted to measure what it purports to measure.

Gronlund (1998, p. 136) writes how performance tasks and the assessments that are built into them usually have the following four characteristics:

1. greater realism of tasks (i.e., more like those in the real world)
2. greater complexity of tasks (i.e., less structured problems that encourage originality and thinking skills and may have multiple solutions)
3. greater time needed for assessment (due to the difficulty of designing tasks, the comprehensive nature of the tasks, and the increased time needed to evaluate the results)
4. greater use of judgment in scoring (due to the complexity of tasks, originality of the responses, and, in some cases, the variety of possible solutions)

Types of Performance Tasks

Gronlund uses the designation *restricted performance* to refer to performance tasks that tend to be highly structured to fit a specific instructional objective (e.g., read aloud a selection of poetry or construct a graph from a given set of data). He uses the term *extended performance* to refer to tasks that are so comprehensive that numerous instructional objectives are involved. Extended performance tasks tend to be less structured and broad in scope. One task could ask students to "assume you are investing $40,000 in the stock market for your college education. Select the stocks, make a record of their value for 30 days, then write a report describing your success and indicating what changes you would make in your portfolio of stocks" (Gronlund, 1998, pp. 136–137). Another extended performance task could ask students to bid on a job to landscape their school. Students could be told they have one week to prepare the following:

1. a written proposal
2. a diagram of the landscape design plan
3. a three-minute videotape on the proposed plan to present to school officials

The extended performance task includes several smaller tasks that can be assessed separately, but they are all part of a bigger task that involves initial and creative problem-solving.

Performance tasks appear in many different forms according to Gronlund (1998, p. 136), but the majority of them fall into the following categories:

1. solving realistic problems (e.g., how to reduce drug use in the United States)
2. oral or psychomotor skills without a product (e.g., giving a speech, speaking a foreign language, using a microscope, repairing an engine)
3. writing or psychomotor skills with a product (e.g., writing a theme, writing a lab report, typing a letter, building a bookcase)

From *Assessment of Student Achievement* by N. E. Gronlund (6th ed.). Copyright © 1998 by Allyn & Bacon. Reprinted by permission.

Probably the key characteristic of performance tasks involves using real-life applications to real-life problems. Performances require students to apply what they have learned—not just fill in a selected-response Scantron test. By demonstrating what they can do, students have a greater probability of transferring the skills they have learned to their lives rather than merely reproducing knowledge for a test.

Performances require students to apply what they have learned.

Performance Tasks and Rubrics

Teachers differentiate the group work by "tiering." Tomlinson and Eidson (2003, p. 190) define tiering as a process of adjusting the degree of difficulty of a question, task, or product to match a student's current readiness level. One way to tier is to develop multiple versions of the task at different levels of difficulty, ensuring that all versions focus on the essential knowledge, understanding, and skills.

Page 79 shows an example of how performance tasks can be designed. Page 100 provides a template to use when designing performance tasks.

Why Performance Tasks?

Advocates of performance tests and performance assessment base their support on a number of factors. Mehrens (1992, as cited in Popham, 1999), a prominent educational measurement specialist, has identified descriptors of three influences he believes contribute to the support for performance assessment. A summary of those influences include:

- *Dissatisfaction with selected-response tests.* Multiple-choice tests ask students to select only a response that calls for recognition on the part of the student but fails to tap higher-order thinking skills like problem solving, synthesis, or independent thinking.
- *Influence of cognitive psychology.* Cognitive psychologists believe students must acquire both content knowledge and procedural knowledge since all cognitive tasks require both kinds of knowledge. Since certain types of procedural knowledge are not assessable via selected-response tests, many cognitive psychologists are calling for performance assessments to emphasize students' acquisition of procedural knowledge.
- *The sometimes harmful instructional impact of conventional tasks.* With the advent of high-stakes tests, teachers tend to teach to the test and the mastery of the domain of skills or knowledge on the test. Because many educators recognize that high-stakes tests will continue to influence what a teacher teaches, they argue that performance assessments would constitute more praiseworthy instructional targets by shifting teachers' instructional activities in more appropriate directions.

Language Arts Performance Task

1. *Illinois Language Arts Goal 3: (Middle/Junior High School):*
   Benchmark 3.C.3a: Compose persuasive writings for a specified audience.
2. *Illinois Language Arts Goal 4: (Middle/Junior High School):*
   Benchmark 4.B.3a: Deliver planned oral presentations using language and vocabulary appropriate to the purpose, message, and audience.

Subject Area: *Language Arts/Health*   **Grade:** *8th Grade*

Task Description: As part of the school's Health Fair Week, the Cancer Prevention Association has asked your class to develop a plan for eliminating all smoking areas from local businesses. The project will include: (1) a statistical analysis of research data; (2) a brochure; (3) an anti-smoking poster; and (4) a five-minute PowerPoint™ presentation selling your ideas to business owners. Be prepared to present your antismoking campaign to members of the Cancer Prevention Association on February 3 at their monthly meeting.

Direct Instruction for Whole Class: The whole class will be involved in the following learning experiences:
- Guest lecture from the school nurse on the effects of secondhand smoke
- Lectures and discussions on the health risks related to smoking
- Readings from articles and textbooks
- Oral presentation techniques
- Statistical analysis of research data

Group Work: Students select one group project.

Group One	**Group Two**	**Group Three**	**Group 4**
Prepare a **statistical analysis** using charts and graphs showing the effects of smoking.	Prepare a **brochure** that depicts health risks related to smoking.	Prepare an **anti-smoking poster** to display in local stores.	Prepare a five-minute **PowerPoint™ presentation** to local business owners.

Individual Work: In addition to the group project, each student will complete two individual assignments:
1. Write a letter to the editor of the local newspaper trying to convince business owners to ban smoking in their establishments.
2. Deliver a five-minute presentation to local business owners at the Chamber of Commerce meeting.

Methods of Assessment:
- Teacher-made test on the health risks related to smoking
- Criteria checklists to assess each of the four group projects
- Checklists and rubrics to assess the letter to the editor and the persuasive speech

Performance Tasks and Rubrics

Performance tasks and authentic assessments help teachers focus their instruction on meaningful tasks and interactive methodology to help students prepare for life. They also provide a systematic way to evaluate skills and procedural knowledge that cannot be measured effectively with multiple-choice formats.

Tomlinson (1999) says that differentiation of instruction is a teacher's response to learners' needs guided by general principles of differentiation such as respectful tasks, flexible grouping, and ongoing assessment and adjustment. Performance tasks help teachers differentiate the content, process, and product according to students' readiness, interests, and learning profiles (p. 15).

The balanced assessment approach calls for a repertoire of assessment tools.

The outcomes, standards, and benchmarks in most courses need to be assessed on the basis of performance. As Gronlund (1998) states, "Although tests can tell us whether students know what to do in a particular situation, performance assessments are needed to evaluate their actual performance skills" (p. 138). Once again, it is evident that one type of assessment is not sufficient to evaluate all the content, knowledge, skills, growth, and performances required of students. The balanced assessment approach calls for a repertoire of assessment tools targeted to measure specific learnings and applications. The key for teachers is to determine which tools work best with which students in which situations.

How Should We Assess Performance Tasks?

Popham's (1999) quote at the beginning of this chapter states "performance assessment typically requires students to respond to a small number of more significant tasks rather than respond to a large number of less significant tasks" (p. 161). This characteristic of performance assessment could be a concern for educators. Since the students perform fewer but more in-depth tasks than they do with conventional paper-and-pencil testing, it is more difficult to generalize accurately what skills the student possesses. Instead of multiple assessments, a student's grade could be based on a single task. Psychometricians, according to Popham, have some difficulties with the "generalizability" of the performance to a student's ability. Because of this dilemma, it is important to choose tasks that optimize the likelihood of accurately generalizing a student's capabilities.

Popham (1999) offers seven evaluative criteria that educators might wish to consider when selecting from existing performance tasks or creating their own:

Evaluative Criteria for Performance-Test Tasks

- *Generalizability.* Is there a high likelihood that the students' performance on the task will generalize to comparable tasks?
- *Authenticity.* Is the task similar to what students might encounter in the real world as opposed to encountering only in school?
- *Multiple foci.* Does the task measure multiple instructional outcomes instead of only one?
- *Teachability.* Do students become more proficient in the tassk as a consequence of a teacher's instructional efforts?
- *Fairness.* Is the task fair to all students? Does the task avoid bias based on such personal characteristics as gender, ethnicity, or socioeconomic status?
- *Feasibility.* Is the task realistically implementable in relation to its cost, space, time, and equipment requirements?
- *Scorability.* Is the task likely to elicit student responses that can be reliably and accurately evaluated?

  From *Classroom Assessment: What Teachers Need to Know* by W. James Popham. Copyright © 1999 by Allyn & Bacon. Reprinted by permission.

It is important to select or create performance tasks that require an in-depth understanding of key concepts, knowledge, and skills.

It is important to select or create performance tasks that are "rich" in terms of the criteria which meet and require an in-depth understanding of key concepts, knowledge, and skills. The philosophy of "less is more" threads through performance tasks. If there are fewer tasks, they need to be of the highest quality. "A few truly important criteria are preferable to a plethora of trifling criteria . . . go for the big ones" (Popham, 1999, p. 168). Parents and students are used to seeing hundreds of worksheets with smiley faces each quarter. It is a major paradigm switch for a teacher to go from assigning thirty grades a working period to assigning only ten grades. Educators must justify the importance of fewer tasks that involve more in-depth learning and convey their rationale to students and parents. It is critical to design meaningful performance tasks that meet Popham's criteria if teachers want to make sure the evaluation is valid—measuring what they intend to measure and what was taught—and reliable; the performance can be replicated with consistency on repeated measures.

Criteria for Checklists

Once the performance task is designed, the next very important step involves developing the criteria to determine the adequacy of the student's performance. Bear in mind that a standard dictionary definition for a criterion is a standard on which a judgment or decision may be based. Popham (1999) explains when teachers set criteria they are trying to make a judgment regarding the adequacy of student responses, and the specific criteria to be used will influence the way a response is scored. If a student is giving a speech, the criteria could include eye contact, gestures, organization, visual aid(s), opening, closing, etc.

It is important to review the standards to see if specific criteria are listed. If the criteria are very vague (e.g., the Illinois benchmark that asks students to "compose persuasive writings for a specific audience,") then the teacher has to generate her own list of criteria for "a letter to the editor." If the criteria are more specific, then the teacher should incorporate the vocabulary and criteria from the benchmark into the checklists and rubrics to ensure validity.

Rubrics

Performance assessments usually focus on the application of knowledge to a real-life experience.

Scoring rubrics support learning. Martin-Kniep (2000) defines a rubric as a rating scale that defines and differentiates levels of performance. Checklists indicate the presence or absence of an attribute. Scoring sheets indicate how many points the attribute is worth. A rubric, however, measures degrees of completeness of attributes; identifies all the needed attributes of quality or development in a process, product, or performance; and defines different levels for each of these attributes (p. 34).

Performance assessments usually focus on the application of knowledge to a real-life experience. For example, identifying the parts of a letter requires factual knowledge, but, writing a letter with a purpose and audience requires a real performance—the act of writing the letter. The criteria for judging students' responses identify the factors to be considered when determining the adequacy of a student's performance. Criteria are often referred to as rubrics, scoring guidelines, and scoring dimensions. Marzano, Marzano, and Pickering (2003) feel that rubrics are an excellent tool to help students understand the learning goals. Teachers provide feedback on the goals in both formative measures throughout the process and summative measures for the final product or performance. The criteria are usually discussed with the students before they prepare their product or presentation. Criteria by themselves provide a guideline for students to follow when preparing their performance, but the indicators of what constitutes a quality performance to attain the standard or earn an A or B are usually described in the rubric. See the chart on the following page for sample criteria for judging performances.

SAMPLE CRITERIA FOR JUDGING PERFORMANCES

Speech
- Organization
- Research
- Opening
- Eye contact
- Gestures

Research Paper
- Outline
- Note cards
- Rough draft
- Thesis statement
- Bibliography

Problem Solving
- Problem Identification
- Possible Solutions
- Solution Analysis
- Evaluations

Videotape
- Focus
- Dialogue
- Content
- Activity

Portfolio
- Cover
- Table of contents
- Evidence of understanding
- Reflective comments
- Goal setting
- Self-evaluation

Journal Entry
- Use of examples
- Dialogue
- Grammar
- Sentence structure
- Figures of speech

Solomon (1998) states that "rubrics are a set of guidelines for distinguishing between performances or products of different quality. . . . They should be based on the results of stated performance standards and be composed of scaled descriptive levels of progress towards the result" (p. 120).

Typically, a numerical scale is used for each criterion. Sometimes the scale points are accompanied by verbal descriptors and even visuals. Some scales contain only verbal descriptors with no numbers. Numerical scales assign points to a continuum of performance levels. According to Herman, Aschbacher, and Winters (1992), the length of the continuum or the number of scale points can vary from three to seven or more. However, a shorter scale will result in a higher percentage agreement and a larger scale will take longer to reach consensus if more than one person is evaluating the performance.

Most educators find that even-numbered scales (e.g., 0–1–2–3 or 1–2–3–4 or 1–2–3–4–5–6) work best because odd-numbered scales (e.g., 1–2–3 or 1–2–3–4–5) tend to cause the evaluator to select the middle number. The even-numbered scales force the evaluator to pick a side—either low or high—with no middle ground for compromise. See sample scales on page 84.

Performance Tasks and Rubrics

TYPES OF SCALES

Numerical Scales

0	1	2	3	4
1	2	3	4	5

A Numerical Scale with Verbal Descriptors

1	2	3	4	5
Weak	Satisfactory	Very Good	Excellent	Superior

Verbal Descriptors

Novice	Adequate	Apprentice	Distinguished
Task not completed	Task partially completed		Task completed

DESCRIPTIVE SCALE

Criterion: Eye Contact During Speech

No Evidence	Minimal Evidence	Partial Evidence	Complete Evidence
Does not look at audience	Looks some of the time at some of the audience	Looks most of the time at most of the audience	Looks all of the time at all of the audience

A Fun Rubric

Creating a rubric to assess student performances could be difficult for teachers and students. It is recommended that, as a first step, teachers work with their students to create a fun rubric in order to understand the process of developing rubrics. Topics for a fun rubric could include school lunches, a pep rally, pizza, movies, a graduation party, a field trip, or any nonacademic topic that students know about. The object of the fun rubric is to practice brainstorming criteria and then to develop indicators for ratings. The following is an example of a fun rubric created by students.

RUBRIC FOR ASSESSING A BIRTHDAY PARTY

Scale: Criteria:	1 "I need to go home and do my homework!"	2 "Can't stay—I've got chores at home."	3 "Can I spend the night?"	4 "Will you adopt me?"
Food	Steamed broccoli and carrots	Mom's tuna fish and potato chip casserole	McDonald's Happy Meal™ (free balloons)	Super deluxe supreme pizza (deep dish)
Gifts	New underwear (K-Mart specials)	School supplies (Mr. Eraserhead)	*Finding Nemo* video	Sponge Bob Square Pants video
Entertainment	My sister's poetry readings (T.S. Eliot)	Lawrence Welk polka contest (accordion rap song)	Prince videotape	Usher (live)
Games	Go Fish! and Slap Jack	Musical chairs to Broadway show tunes	Virtual reality headsets	"Full-Contact Twister" (no chaperones)

Adapted from Burke, K.A., Fogarty, R., and Belgrad, S., *The Portfolio Connection Training Manual,* 2nd ed. © 2004 by Pearson Education, Inc. Used with permission of LessonLab, Glenview, IL.

It is recommended that teachers work with their students to create a fun rubric in order to understand the process.

Performance Tasks and Rubrics

Using a Performance Rubric

Once students become familiar with the format of a performance rubric, they understand how to use the rubric to assess their products and performances. Students benefit from rubrics because they identify the attributes of quality work. Rubrics help the students monitor their own progress in meeting or exceeding the standards.

As Martin-Kniep (2000) says, "Rubrics are also helpful to other stakeholders because they enable teachers to justify and validate grades, and they allow people such as parents, supervisors, and support staff to see teachers' criteria for judging students' work. Because they remove the mystery from the attributes of quality work, rubrics often lead to an overall increase in the quality of students' work (p. 39).

Following is a performance rubric for assessing a speech.

RUBRIC FOR ASSESSING A SPEECH

Performance Task: *Students will present a five-minute persuasive speech.*
Goal/Standard: *Speak effectively using language appropriate to the situation and audience.*

SCALE: CRITERIA:	1 Not Yet	2 Student Council Elections	3 The Senate Floor	4 President Debates
Organization				
• Hook	None	Introduces topic	Grabs attention	Electrifies audience
• Transitions	None	Uses words to link ideas	Makes key connections between ideas	Smooth flow of ideas
• Closure	None	Lacks interest	Referred to introduction	Powerful and dramatic
Content				
• Accuracy	3 or more factual errors	2 factual errors	1 factual error	All information is correct
• Documentation	No sources cited	1 source cited	2 sources cited	3 or more sources cited
• Quotations	No quotes	1 quote to support case	2 quotes to support case	3 key quotes to prove case
Delivery				
• Eye contact	Read speech	Looks at some people some of the time	Looks at some people all of the time	Looks at all of the people all of the time
• Volume	Could not be heard	Could be heard by people in front	Could be heard by most people	Could be heard clearly by all people
• Gestures	None	Used a few gestures	Used some gestures appropriately	Used many appropriate gestures effectively
Visual Aid				
• Graphics	None	Minimal	Colorful	Creative graphics that enhance speech
• Appeal	None	Little visual appeal	Captures our attention	Visually stimulates audience
• Relevance	None	Minimal relationship to topic	Relates specifically to topic	Relates and reinforces topic

Student Involvement

One of the most powerful instructional tools to help students internalize the criteria and recognize quality work is to have students develop the criteria for the performance assessment with the teacher. The teacher shows examples of work from different levels and then asks the students to brainstorm the criteria that are essential to the performance task.

After the students identify the criteria and, in some cases, demonstrate or gather more examples to make sure every student understands the expectations, the class selects four or five criteria at a time in order to focus on key elements. The number of criteria expand as the students become more proficient or when new criteria replace ones that have been mastered. Students presenting their first persuasive speech should not be expected to achieve the same level as a Martin Luther King, Jr.; the expectations should simply correlate with the benchmarks of the grade level. Educators need to progress at a speed that is developmentally appropriate and allows students to undertake a novel challenge that is neither too easy nor too difficult.

Haberman (1991, as cited in Williams, 1996) believes that good teaching occurs when students in classrooms are

- involved with issues they regard as vital concerns;
- helped to see major concepts, big ideas, and general principles and are not merely engaged in the pursuit of isolated facts;
- involved in real-life experiences;
- redoing, polishing, or perfecting their work; and
- involved in the technology of information access (p. 83).

The reality of performance tasks is that they represent an alternative to traditional paper-and-pencil tests, and that they often are more authentic—that is, reflective of the types of tasks students will be called upon to perform in the real world. Performance tasks must be rigorous and suitable tasks, and the scoring procedures should isolate "appropriate evaluative criteria and spell out the scoring scale for each criterion" (Popham, 1999, p. 177).

Another reality of performance tasks is that they take much more time to construct and score than a selected-response Scantron test. The time, however, is time well spent. The students' performances will demonstrate their in-depth learning. In addition, feedback provided from their self-assessment using the rubric will provide valuable feedback to the teacher.

The reality of performance tasks is that they often are more authentic.

Performance Tasks and Rubrics

The use of performance tasks and rubrics demonstrates the power of integrated instruction with evaluation. It is impossible to know where instruction stops and assessment begins. In fact, instruction and assessment are so closely correlated in today's classroom that they literally become the intersection of learning.

Examples

The following examples show how teachers begin with the targeted standard in the individual work in the Performance Task Unit.

The targeted standard does not appear in the groupwork since the groups all do different tasks. Each individual student needs to show he or she can meet the standards. The examples show how teachers start with the standard and then move to the criteria checklist that shows students what is required, and then moves to the rubric that shows level of quality. Some benchmarks do not give lots of criteria so the teacher generates her own. Others provide specific criteria that must be embedded in the checklist. Regardless, teachers have to add criteria to help students understand the steps necessary to meet the standard.

EXAMPLE

Illinois English Language Arts

State Goal 3:

Write to communicate for a variety of purposes.

Learning Standard 3c:

Communicate ideas in writing to accomplish a variety of purposes.

Middle/Junior High 3.C.3a:

Compose narrative, informative, and persuasive writings (e.g., in addition to previous writings, literature, reviews, instructions, news articles, correspondence) for a specified audience.

From Illinois State Board of Education (1997). *Illinois Learning Standards,* p. 9. Springfield, IL: Author.

Performance Tasks and Rubrics

Teacher-Generated Criteria for Letter to the Editor

(Unclustered)

- Facts

- Statistics

- Logic

- Arguments

- Examples

- Quotations

- Grammar

- Spelling

- Mechanics

- Letter format

- Salutation

- Inside address

- Closing

- Signature

Letter to the Editor Clustered Checklist

Illinois Language Arts Standard: 3.C.3a: Middle/Junior High School
Benchmark: Compose narrative, informative, and persuasive writings (e.g., in addition to previous writings, literature reviews, instructions, news articles, correspondence) for a specified audience.

Clustered Checklist	Not Yet 0	Some Evidence 1
Accuracy of Information		
• Facts		
• Statistics		
Persuasiveness		
• Logic		
• Examples		
• Quotations		
Organization		
• Topic sentence		
• Support sentences		
• Concluding sentence		
Usage		
• Grammar		
• Sentence structure		
• Transitions		
Mechanics		
• Capitalization		
• Punctuation		
• Spelling		
Letter Format		
• Date		
• Inside address		
• Salutation		
• Body		
• Closing		
• Signature		

Comments:

Scale
18–20 = A
16–17 = B
14–15 = C
Not Yet

Total Points: _____

Final Grade: _____

Performance Tasks and Rubrics

EXAMPLE

Letter to the Editor Rubric

Assignment: *Write a letter to the editor of your local paper persuading readers to take a stand on a controversial issue.*

Illinois Language Arts Benchmark: 3.C.3a. Middle/Junior High School: *Compose persuasive writings for a specified audience.*

Scale: Criteria:	1 Rejected By Church Bulletin Committee	2 Published in High School Newspaper	3 Published in Local Newspaper	4 Published in *The New York Times*	Score
Accuracy of Information • Facts • Statistics	3 or more factual errors	2 factual errors	1 factual error	All information is accurate and current	__ x 4 __ (16)
Persuasiveness • Logic • Examples • Quotations	• Illogical • No examples • No quotations	• Faulty logic • 1 example • 1 quotation	• Logical arguments • 2 examples • 2 quotations	• Logical and convincing arguments • 3 examples • 3 quotations	__ x 4 __ (16)
Organization • Topic sentence • Support sentences • Concluding sentence	• Includes 2 elements • Fragmented	• Includes 2 elements • Lacks coherence	• Includes all 3 elements • Logical • Coherent	• Includes all 3 elements • Logical • Coherent • Powerful concluding sentence	__ x 4 __ (16)
Usage • Grammar • Sentence structure • Transitions	4 or more errors (distracts from arguments)	2–3 errors (weakens case)	1 error (structure reinforces arguments)	No errors (structure reinforces arguments and convinces reader)	__ x 4 __ (16)
Mechanics • Capitalization • Punctuation • Spelling	4 or more errors (destroys credibility)	2–3 errors (weakens case)	1 error (careless proofreading)	Accurate mechanics (polished and professional)	__ x 4 __ (16)
Letter Format • Date • Inside address • Salutation • Body • Closing • Signature	• Includes 3 elements • Out of order • Incorrect punctuation	• Includes 4 elements • In order • Incorrect punctuation	• Includes 5 elements • Correct order • Correct punctuation	• Includes all 6 elements • Correct order • Correct punctuation	__ x 4 __ (16)

Students Comments (4 points): _____

Scale
A = 92–100
B = 84–91
C = 77–83
D = 70–76

Total Points: _____

96

(4 points for comments)   100

Final Grade: _____

Adapted from Burke, K.A. (1999). *The Mindful School: How to Assess Authentic Learning Training Manual*, 3rd ed. Arlington Heights, IL: SkyLight Training and Publishing. Reprinted with permission of LessonLab, Glenview, IL.

Illinois English Language Arts

State Goal 4:

Listen and speak effectively in a variety of situations.

Learning Standard 4b:

Speak effectively using language appropriate to the situation and audience.

Middle/Junior High School Benchmark 4.B.3a:

Deliver planned oral presentations using language and vocabulary appropriate to the purpose, message, and audience; provide details and support information that clarify main ideas; and use visual aids and contemporary technology as support.

Adapted from Illinois State Board of Education (1997). *Illinois Learning Standards,* p. 9. Springfield, IL: Author.

 EXAMPLE

Unclustered Criteria for an Oral Presentation

- Language

- Vocabulary

- Purpose

- Message

- Audience

- Support information

- Main ideas

- Visual aids

- Contemporary technology

State Goal 4—Language Arts, Illinois Benchmark 4.B.3a

EXAMPLE

Oral Presentation Clustered Checklist

Illinois English Language Arts Standard 4.B:
Speak effectively using language appropriate to the situation and audience.

Middle/Junior High School Benchmark: 4.B.3a:
Deliver planned oral presentations using language and vocabulary appropriate to the purpose, message, audience; provide details and supporting information that clarify main ideas and use visual aids and contemporary technology as support.

Criteria/Performance Indicators:	Not Yet 0	Some Evidence ✓
Language and Vocabulary		
• Appropriate to the purpose		
• Appropriate to the message		
• Appropriate to the audience		
Information to Support and Clarify the Main Idea		
• Details		
• Examples		
• Statistics		
• Quotes		
• Anecdotes		
Visual Aids (select two)		
• Graphic organizer		
• Picture		
• Poster		
• Pamphlet		
• Costume		
Technology (select two)		
• Transparencies		
• Slides		
• PowerPoint™		
• Videotape		
• Digital pictures		

Comments:

Scale
18–20 = A
16–17 = B
14–15 = C
Not Yet

Total Points: _____

Final Grade: _____

Performance Tasks and Rubrics

EXAMPLE

Oral Presentation Rubric

Illinois English Language Arts Standard 4.B:
Speak effectively using language appropriate to the situation and audience.

Middle/Junior High School Benchmark: 4.B.3a:
Deliver planned oral presentations using language and vocabulary appropriate to the purpose, message, and audience; provide details and supporting information that clarify main ideas; and use visual aids and contemporary technology as support.

SCALE: CRITERIA:	1 **Practiced in Front of Mirror** **(Novice)**	2 **Enrolled in Toastmaster Course** **(In Progress)**	3 **Voted Class President** **(Meets Standards)**	4 **Nominated for an Oscar** **(Exceeds Standards)**
Language and Vocabulary • Appropriate to purpose • Appropriate to message • Appropriate to audience	Language and vocabulary appropriate to purpose	Language and vocabulary appropriate to • purpose • message	Language and vocabulary appropriate to • purpose • message • audience	Language and vocabulary enhances • purpose • message • audience
Support and Clarification Main Idea • Details • Examples • Statistics • Quotes • Anecdotes	Limited use of details to support main idea	Effective use of appropriate • details • examples	Effective use of appropriate • details • examples • statistics	Effective use of • details • examples • statistics • quotes • anecdotes
Visual Aids • Graphic organizer • Picture • Poster • Prop • Pamphlet • Costume	No visual aids used in presentation	Use of *one* visual aid to support main idea	• Use of *two* visual aids to support main idea • Kept the attention of the audience	• Use of *two or more* visual aids • Support main idea • Kept the attention of the audience • Excited the audience
Technology • Transparencies • Slides • PowerPoint™ • Videotape • Digital pictures	No use of technology	• Use of *one* technology tool • Supported main idea	• Use of *two* technology tools • Supported main idea • Kept the attention of the audience	• Use of *two or more* contemporary technology tools • Clarified main idea • Inspired the audience to action!

Student Comment:

Teacher Comment:

Scale
15–16 = A
12–14 = B
8–11 = C
Not Yet

ON YOUR OWN

Clustered Criteria Checklist

Standard: _____

Assignment: _____

Criteria/Performance Indicators	Not Yet 0	Some Evidence 1
•		
•		
•		
•		
•		
•		
•		
•		
•		
•		
•		
•		
•		
•		
•		

Adapted from Burke, K.A., Fogarty, R., & Belgrad, S. (2002). *The Portfolio Connection: Student Work Linked to Standards*, 2nd ed. Arlington Heights, IL: SkyLight Professional Development, Inc. Reprinted with permission of LessonLab, Glenview, IL.

Performance Tasks and Rubrics

Rubric Template

Performance: _____

Objectives/Standards: _____

	SCALE:	1	2	3	4
CRITERIA:					
•					
•					
•					
•					
•					
•					
•					
•					
•					
•					
•					
•					

Performance Task

Design a Travel Brochure for a Country

Standards
1. Demonstrate competence in the general skills and strategies of the writing process.
2. Gather and use information for research purposes.

Benchmarks
Writes pieces that convey an intended purpose (to describe, to explain, to market). Writes for an intended audience (tourists).

Travel Brochure for a Country
You work for the department of tourism for the country you selected for your research project. Your task is to design an attractive and informative brochure to entice tourists to visit your country. You must include a creative cover, a brief history of the country, major attractions, weather information, the cost of the trip, and testimonials from visitors to your country. Be prepared to present your final brochure to the executive director of your country's tourism department on September 6 at their monthly meeting.

Rubric to Assess Travel Brochure

Criteria/Scale	1	2	3	4
Cover	No evidence	• 2 colors • No graphics	• 2 colors • 1 graphic	• 3 colors • 2 graphics
History	No evidence	• 3–4 inaccuracies • Poorly written	• 1–2 inaccuracies • Few mistakes	• No inaccuracies • Coherent and interesting
Attractions	No evidence	• 1–2 attractions • Inaccurate descriptions	• 3–4 attractions • Accurate descriptions	• 5–6 attractions • Vivid descriptions that attract visitors
Weather	No evidence	• No temperatures • Missing a season	• Temperatures given for all seasons	• Temperatures given for all seasons • Clothing recommendations included
Cost	No evidence	• Travel • Hotel	• Travel • Hotel • Dining	• Travel • Hotel • Dining • Recreation
Testimonials	No evidence	• 1–2 quotes • Vague or boring	• 3–4 quotes • Specific and interesting	• 3–4 quotes • Vivid and motivating • Famous personalities

Performance Tasks and Rubrics

Performance Task Template

Subject Area: _____ **Grade Level:** _____

Learning Standards: _____

Task Description:

Direct Instruction for Whole Class: The whole class will be involved in the following learning experiences:

Group Work: Students may select their group and their task.

  Group One   Group Two   Group Three   Group Four

Individual Work: In addition to the group project, each student will complete the following individual assignments:

Methods of Assessment:

EXAMPLES

PRIMARY

RUBRIC FOR ORAL READING

First Grade

Student: _____

Book: _____

Performance Task: _____

Book 1	Book 2	Book 3	Book 4
Knows only beginning sounds of words and a few words.	Knows how to read some words in text with help.	Knows how to read most words with minimal help.	Knows how to read entire book independently.

Score	Date
_____	September _____
_____	January _____
_____	June _____

Signed: _____

MIDDLE SCHOOL

WEIGHTED COMPUTER LITERACY SCALE

Name: _____ Date: _____

Topic: Hypercard

Type of Assessment: ☐ Self   ☐ Group   ☐ Teacher

Score (1–5)   1 — 2 — 3 — 4
   Low   High

Directions: Circle the score for each indicator.

Terminology   Score: ___ x 8 = ___ (32)
- Understands key functions   1 2 3 4
- Relates one function to others 1 2 3 4
- Uses to solve problems   1 2 3 4
- Correct spelling   1 2 3 4
- Appropriate to level   1 2 3 4

Organization   Score: ___ x 7 = ___ (28)
- Easy to complex   1 2 3 4
- Each card complete   1 2 3 4
- Uses graphics   1 2 3 4
- Key ideas covered   1 2 3 4
- Supportive data included   1 2 3 4

Creativity   Score: ___ x10 = ___ (40)
- Color   1 2 3 4
- Style   1 2 3 4
- Pattern   1 2 3 4
- Appropriate use of language   1 2 3 4
- Multiple uses   1 2 3 4

Scale: 93–100 = A   78–86 = C   Total Score: _____
        87–92 = B   70–77 = D   (100)

Comments:

(Courtesy of Kathy Bartley and Jeanne Lipman, Gabbard Institute, 1994.)

HIGH SCHOOL

HOLISTIC ORAL PRESENTATION RUBRIC

Name: _____ Date: _____

Subject: _____ Final Grade: _____

5	Subject is addressed clearly Speech is loud enough and easy to understand Good eye contact Visual aid is used effectively Well-organized
4	Subject is addressed adequately Speech has appropriate volume Eye contact is intermittent Visual aid helps presentations Good organization
3	Subject is addressed adequately Speech volume is erratic Student reads notes—erratic eye contact Visual aid does not enhance speech Speech gets off track in places
2	Speech needs more explanation Speech is difficult to understand at times Lack of adequate eye contact Poor visual aid Lack of organization
1	Speech does not address topic Speech cannot be heard Very little eye contact No visual aid No organization

Scale: 5 = A; 4 = B; 3 = C; 2 = D; 1 = Not Yet
General Comments:

COLLEGE

WEIGHTED WRITING RUBRIC

Name: _____ Date: _____

Piece of Writing: _____

Score (1–5)   Score: 1   2   3   4
                         Low   High

	Score	
CONTENT (4) • evidence of reason • key ideas covered • appropriate quotes • supportive statistics • topic addressed	Score ____	x 8 = ___ (32)
ORGANIZATION (4) • creative introduction • thesis statement • appropriate support statements • effective transition	Score ____	x 8 = ___ (32)
USAGE (4) • correct subject-verb agreement • no run-ons, fragments, or comma splices • correct verb tense • mix of simple and complex sentences	Score ____	x 6 = ___ (24)
MECHANICS (4) • few or no misspellings • correct use of punctuation • correct use of capitalization	Score ____	x 2 = ___ (12)

TOTAL SCORE: _____

Scale: 93–100=A, 87–92=B, 78–86=C   (100)
Comments:

Performance Tasks and Rubrics

Performance Tasks and Rubrics

1. What are three advantages of using the performance task unit plan to introduce important standards and curriculum?

    a. _____

    _____

    b. _____

    _____

    c. _____

    _____

2. How do you feel about rubrics? Rate yourself and explain why you feel the way you do.

A rubric is a rubric is a rubric.

Show me the Scantron!	Rubrics are our friends!	Rubrics rock!	Rubrics are my life!

Explanation:

TEACHER-MADE TESTS

CHAPTER 6

"While large-scale standardized tests may appear to have great influence at specific times . . . Without question, teachers are the drivers of the assessment systems that determine the effectiveness of schools."

—STIGGINS, 1994, P. 438

Teacher-Made Tests

What Are Teacher-Made Tests?

Teacher-made tests are written or oral assessments that are not commercially produced or standardized—in other words, they are tests a teacher designs specifically for his or her students. *Testing* refers to any kind of school activity that results in some type of mark or comment being entered in a checklist, grade book, or anecdotal record. The term *test,* however, refers to a more structured oral or written evaluation of student achievement. Examinations are tests that are school scheduled, tend to cover more of the curriculum, and count more than other forms of evaluation (Board of Education for the City of Etobicoke, 1987). Teacher-made tests consist of a variety of formats, including matching items, fill-in-the-blank items, true-false questions, or essays.

Teacher-made tests can be important parts of the teaching and learning process if they are integrated into daily classroom teaching.

Tests can be important parts of the teaching and learning process if they are integrated into daily classroom teaching and are constructed to be part of the learning process—not just the culminating event. They allow students to see their own progress and allow teachers to make adjustments to their instruction on a daily basis. "But one of the most serious problems of evaluation is the fact that a primary means of assessment—the test itself—is often severely flawed or misused" (Hills, 1991, p. 541).

Constructing a good teacher-made test is very time consuming and difficult; moreover, it is hard to understand why something so essential to the learning process has been virtually ignored in teacher preservice or inservice training. Teachers have sometimes relied too heavily on commercially produced tests that don't always correlate to what the teacher has taught. Moreover, some teacher-made tests don't always provide opportunities for students to demonstrate what they have learned and what they can do.

One of the problems with teacher-made tests is their emphasis on lower-level thinking. A study conducted by the Cleveland Public Schools (Fleming and Chambers, 1983, as cited in Stiggins, 1985) examined over 300 teacher-made, paper-and-pencil tests. The results of the study found that teachers appeared to need training in how to do the following:

1. plan and write longer tests,
2. write unambiguous paper-and-pencil test items, and
3. measure skills beyond the recall of facts (Stiggins, 1985, p. 72).

The research also found that teachers often overlooked quality control factors like establishing written criteria for performances or planning scoring procedures in advance. Wiggins (1989) notes that "course-specific tests also have glaring weaknesses, not only because they are often too low level and content heavy. They are rarely designed to be authentic tests of intellectual ability; as with standardized tests, teacher-designed finals are usually intended to be quickly read and scored" (p. 73).

In addition, many teacher-made tests emphasize verbal/linguistic intelligence, and poor readers are at a disadvantage no matter how much content they know. Teacher-made tests do not carry the same importance as standardized tests in public relations between the school and the community. Even though many of them have the same objective-style format that allows for easy comparisons, they are not seen as reliable and valid. Teacher-made tests are often subject to question because they differ greatly from class to class; their quality is open to debate. Stiggins (1994) notes that although standardized, large-scale assessments command all the media attention, it's the day-to-day classroom assessments that have the greatest impact on student learning. "Nearly all the assessment events that take place in a student's life happen at the behest of the teacher. They align most closely with day-to-day instruction and are most influential in terms of their contribution to student, teacher, and parent decision making" (p. 438).

Teacher-made tests are often subject to question because they differ greatly from class to class; their quality is open to debate.

Since colleges of education are just beginning to require teachers to take courses in assessment, many teachers have entered the classroom with very little training in how to create meaningful tests. They either remember the types of tests they took as students or they model the tests on ones provided by their fellow teachers or in workbooks. Unfortunately, most of the tests teachers took as students were multiple-choice, recall tests that covered content. Teachers have had very little practice constructing problem-solving situations on tests to measure the application of skills and higher-order thinking.

Why Do We Need Teacher-Made Tests?

Even though parents and the media value published test scores, most teachers do not rely on standardized tests to tell them what their students know and don't know. Standardized tests occur so infrequently that one aggregate score is not very helpful in determining future instructional goals. Teacher-made tests, however, allow teachers to make decisions that keep instruction moving. Teachers can make changes immediately to meet the needs of their students.

Teacher-Made Tests

"[Teachers] rely most heavily on assessments provided as part of instructional materials and assessments they design and construct themselves—and very little on standardized tests or test scores" (Stiggins, 1985, p. 69).

The key to teacher-made tests is to make them a part of assessment—not separate from it. Tests should be instructional and ongoing. Rather than being "after-the-fact" to find out what students did not learn, they should be more "before-the-fact" to target essential learnings and standards. Popham (1999) warns that teacher-made tests should not be instructional afterthoughts. *They should be prepared prior to* instruction in order for the teacher to target appropriate instructional activities for students. "Assessment instruments prepared prior to instruction operationalize a teacher's instructional intentions. . . . The better you understand where you're going, the more efficiently you can get there" (p. 12).

The key to teacher-made tests is to make them a part of assessment—not separate from it.

Teachers also need to make adjustments in their tests for the various learning styles, multiple intelligences, and learning problems of the students in their classes. It would be impossible to address every student's needs on every test, but efforts should be made to construct tests that motivate students to learn, provide choices, and make allowances for individual differences.

Multiple Intelligences

Gardner's theory of multiple intelligences (reviewed in chapter three) calls for multiple assessments for the multiple intelligences. An effective teacher-made test should address more than one or two intelligences. Teachers who include strategies and tools such as graphic organizers, student choice, and opportunities for oral answers meet the needs of their diverse students.

Learning Modalities

Teachers need to construct tests that can be adjusted for students' learning modalities and to make modifications for at-risk students. Frender (1990) defines learning modalities as ways of using sensory information to learn. Three of the five senses are primarily used in learning, storing, and recalling information. Because students learn from and communicate best with someone who shares their dominant modality, it is important for teachers to know the characteristics of their students so that they can at least alter their instructional styles and tests to match the learning styles of all the students.

Frender identified many characteristics of the three styles of learning. The Types of Learners chart below lists the characteristics that could most likely influence student test-taking skills.

TYPES OF LEARNERS

Visual Learners	Auditory Learners	Kinesthetic Learners
mind sometimes strays during verbal activities	talks to self	in motion most of the time
organized in approach to tasks	easily distracted	reading is not a priority
likes to read	has difficulty with written directions	poor speller
usually a good speller	likes to be read to	likes to solve problems by physically walking through them
memorizes by seeing graphics and pictures	memorizes by steps in a sequence	enjoys handling objects
finds verbal instructions difficult	enjoys listening activities	enjoys doing activities

(Adapted from Frender, 1990, p. 25.)

Authentic tests can celebrate diversity by allowing students a wide variety of ways to demonstrate what they know and what they can do.

Modifications for Students With Special Needs

With the movement toward inclusive classrooms, teachers need to be able to meet the needs of students with learning disabilities, behavior exceptionalities, physical exceptionalities, and intellectual exceptionalities. In addition, as today's society is a "salad bowl" of many ethnic groups, teacher-made tests must allow opportunities for students whose first language is not English to succeed. Many schools have now detracked, thereby merging all levels of students (gifted, average, remedial) into one inclusive class. It would be impossible to use one objective test to measure the growth and development of all students. Authentic tests can celebrate diversity by allowing students a wide variety of ways to demonstrate what they know and what they can do. Teacher-made tests can be constructed to meet the needs of all students by providing many opportunities to measure what students can do instead of just measuring their ability to read, write, and take tests.

Teacher-Made Tests

The following modifications can be made to help ensure success on tests for all students, especially those with special needs who are most at risk of failing:

1. Read instructions orally.
2. Rephrase oral instructions if needed.
3. Ask students to repeat directions to make sure they understand.
4. Monitor carefully to make sure all students understand directions for the test.
5. Provide alternative evaluations (e.g., oral testing, use of tapes, test given in another room, dictation).
6. Provide a clock so students can monitor themselves.
7. Give examples of each type of question (oral and written).
8. Leave enough space for answers.
9. Use visual demonstrations.
10. Use white paper because colored paper is sometimes distracting.
11. Do not crowd or clutter the test.
12. Give choices.
13. Go from concrete to abstract.
14. Don't deduct for spelling or grammar on tests.
15. Use some take-home tests.
16. Provide manipulative experiences whenever possible.
17. Allow students to use notes and textbooks during some tests (open book tests).
18. Allow students to write down key math or science formulas (so that students are not penalized for poor memory).
19. Include visuals like graphic organizers on tests.
20. Give specific point values for each group of questions.
21. List criteria for essay questions.
22. Provide immediate feedback on all tests.
23. Allow students to correct mistakes and/or to retake tests to improve scores and understand what they didn't understand on the first test.

(Adapted from Board of Education for the City of Etobicoke, 1987, pp. 204–214.)

How Can We Design Better Teacher-Made Tests?

Most teachers will not have time to rewrite all their tests to conform to the guidelines suggested above. However, it is important to make sure new tests are designed to meet student needs—and truly reflect learning. Teachers should teach to the authentic test, therefore, students should also be brought into the test-making process. They can help construct meaningful tests based on essential learnings. Brown (1989) recommends that teachers draw students into the development of tests. He maintains that nothing helps a person master a subject better than having to ask and debate fundamental questions about what is most important about that subject—and how someone could tell if he or she has mastered it. Students focus on "what's on the test," therefore quality tests improve learning.

Guidelines for Teacher-Made Tests

The following guidelines may help in the construction of better teacher-made tests:

Students should be brought into the test-making process.

1. Create the test before beginning the unit.
2. Make sure the test is correlated to course objectives or learning standards and benchmarks.
3. Give clear directions for each section of the test.
4. Arrange the questions from simple to complex.
5. Give point values for each section (e.g., true-false [2 points each]).
6. Vary the question types (true-false, fill-in-the-blank, multiple-choice, essay, matching). Limit the amount of questions to ten per type.
7. Group question types together.
8. Type or print clearly. (Leave space between questions to facilitate easy reading and writing.)
9. Make sure the appropriate reading level is used.
10. Include a variety of visual, oral, and kinesthetic tasks.
11. Make allowances for students with special needs.
12. Give students some choice in the questions they select (e.g., a choice of graphic organizers or essay questions).
13. Vary levels of questions by using the three-story intellect verbs to cover gathering, processing, and application questions. (See pages 113–114.)
14. Provide a grading scale so students know what score constitutes a certain grade (e.g., 93–100 = A; 85–92 = B; 75–84 = C; 70–74 = D; Below 70 = Not Yet!).
15. Give sufficient time for all students to finish. (The teacher should be able to work through the test in one-third to one-half the time given students.)

Teacher-Made Tests

Constructing Effective Tests

One way teachers can construct better teacher-made tests is to consider the types of questions that should be included on a test. Obviously, it is important to select test items that measure whether students have achieved the significant learning objectives, benchmarks, or standards that have been targeted.

It is important to select test items that measure whether students have achieved the significant learning objectives, benchmarks, or standards.

TIPS FOR CONSTRUCTING TEST QUESTIONS

True-False Items
- Avoid absolute words like *all, never,* and *always.*
- Make sure items are clearly true or false rather than ambiguous.
- Limit true-false questions to ten.
- Consider asking students to make false questions true to encourage higher-order thinking.

Matching Items
- Limit the list to between five and ten items.
- Use homogeneous lists. (Don't mix names with dates.)
- Give clear instructions. (Write the letter, number, etc.)
- Give more choices than there are questions.

Multiple-Choice Items
- State the main idea in the core or stem of the question.
- Use reasonable incorrect choices. (Avoid ridiculous choices.)
- Make options the same length (nothing very long or very short).
- Include multiple correct answers (a and b, all of the above).

Completion Items
- Structure for a brief, specific answer for each item.
- Avoid passages lifted directly from text (emphasis on memorization).
- Use blanks of equal length.
- Avoid multiple blanks that sometimes make a sentence too confusing.

Essay Items
- Avoid all-encompassing questions ("Discuss" is ambiguous. "Tell all you know about a subject is clean.").
- Define criteria for evaluation.
- Give point value.
- Use some higher-order thinking verbs like *predict* or *compare and contrast* rather than all recall verbs like *list* and *name.*

(Adapted from Board of Education for the City of Etobicoke, 1987, pp. 112–187.)

Essays, graphic organizers, oral performances, and artistic presentations measure meaningful learning and can be included on teacher-made tests. Because of time constraints, however, many teachers choose to use objective-style questions. Objective-style questions have highly specific, predetermined answers that require a short response.

Objective-style questions include the following:

1. multiple choice
2. true-false
3. matching
4. short response

Even though objective-style questions play a role in the assessment process, they, like standardized tests, must be put in the proper perspective. "Evaluation should be a learning experience for both the student and the teacher. However, objective-style testing is frequently ineffective as a learning experience for either the student or the teacher because objective-style questions too often require only the recall of facts and do not allow the student to display thinking processes or the teacher to observe them" (Board of Education for the City of Etobicoke, 1987, p. 156).

Objective-style questions can play a role in the assessment, but they must be put in the proper perspective.

OBJECTIVE TYPES OF EVALUATION

A well-developed objective test . . .

Advantages	Disadvantages
• can evaluate skills quickly and efficiently	• requires mostly recall of facts
• can prevent students from "writing around" the answer	• does not allow students to demonstrate writing skills
• can prevent students' grades from being influenced by writing skills, spelling, grammar, and neatness	• often requires a disproportionate amount of reading (penalizes poor readers)
• can be easily analyzed (item analysis)	• can be ambiguous and confusing (especially to younger students)
• prevents biased grading by teacher	• usually has a specific, predetermined answer
• can be used for diagnostic or pretest purposes	• can be very time consuming to construct
• can be given to large groups	• promotes guessing
	• is often used year after year despite differing needs of students

(Adapted from the Board of Education for the City of Etobicoke, 1987, pp. 157–158.)

Gardner (as cited in Scherer, 1999), states, "I am not a fan of short-answer tests because they can't really assess understanding. The world does not come with four choices, the last one being 'none of the above'." He also says that the more time we spend trying to isolate bits of information that lend themselves to assessment in a short answer instrument, "the less time that we have to present materials that are rich in content and that can engender understanding" (p. 13).

A good evaluation program does not have to include objective-style tests; however, if it does, the questions should be well-constructed and the objective-style tests should be balanced by other authentic assessments.

Objective-style tests should be balanced by other authentic assessments.

Misconceptions About Objective Tests

Often, critics of authentic assessment point out that evaluating products, performances, and portfolios is too "subjective," and that teachers could assign a grade because they liked or didn't like a student or could base the grade upon outside variables like neatness, attendance, or behavior. These same critics point to objective tests being fairer or more valid and reliable. Since most well-written, selected-response test items frame challenges that allow for just one best answer or a limited set of acceptable answers, it leads to the "objective" evaluation of responses as being right or wrong. However, Stiggins (1994) warns that when the teacher selects the test items for inclusion in the final test, he or she is making a subjective judgment as to the meaning and importance of the material to be tested. ". . . all assessments, regardless of their format, involve judgment on the part of the assessor. Therefore, all assessments reflect the biases of that assessor" (p. 103).

Teachers should examine both the advantages and disadvantages of objective-style tests and then determine the role they will play in the evaluation process.

Questioning Techniques and Three-Story Intellect Verbs

Marzano, Pickering, and Pollock (2005) identified nine families of strategies that significantly increase student achievement. The first family deals with finding similarities and differences, specifically comparing and contrasting, classifying, metaphors, and analogies.

Teachers can include questions on tests that require students to compare and contrast, an analysis skill of finding similarities and differences. Students are asked to compare the attributes that are alike, but contrast the ones that are different. Classifying is another important skill. Classifying organizes by sorting according to similarities. Things that have similar attributes are separated from those that don't share these similarities. Pete and Fogarty (2003, p. 5) state that "classification is like an egg carton: both have compartments that separate and divide, providing a specified place for each thing and a unifying element that brings the individual items into a connected whole."

A good teacher-made test includes verbs from all three stories of the intellect.

Bellanca and Fogarty (1986) have created a graphic based on Bloom's Taxonomy called the Three-Story Intellect (see p. 114) to show what verbs teachers can use when they ask questions. First-story verbs like *count, describe,* and *match* ask students to *gather* or *recall* information. Second-story verbs like *reason, compare,* and *analyze* ask students to *process* information. And third-story verbs like *evaluate, imagine,* and *speculate* ask students to *apply* information. An effective teacher-made test includes verbs from all three stories of the intellect. Many teachers use this graphic as a guide when they ask questions in class and when they create teacher-made tests that encourage higher-order thinking.

A self-check teachers can use to evaluate the effectiveness of teacher-made tests and commercially made tests appears on page 116. The Three-Story Intellect Verbs Review on page 117 provides a method to analzye tests to determine how many questions address each of the three levels of learning—gathering, processing, and applying. A well-balanced test should include questions from all levels to assess students' recall of factual information, their ability to process that information and, most important, their ability to apply that information by doing something with it. Stiggins (1994) observes that it is teachers and the assessments they create that have the most impact on student learning and drive the assessment systems in schools.

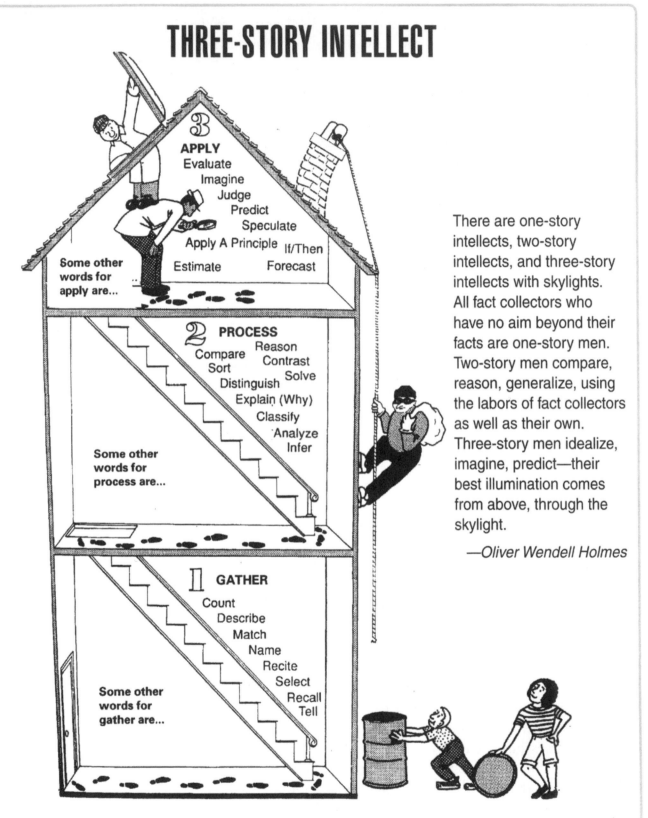

THREE-STORY INTELLECT

3 APPLY
Evaluate
Imagine
Judge
Predict
Speculate
Apply A Principle If/Then
Estimate Forecast

Some other words for apply are...

2 PROCESS
Reason
Compare Contrast
Sort Solve
Distinguish
Explain (Why)
Classify
Analyze
Infer

Some other words for process are...

1 GATHER
Count
Describe
Match
Name
Recite
Select
Recall
Tell

Some other words for gather are...

There are one-story intellects, two-story intellects, and three-story intellects with skylights. All fact collectors who have no aim beyond their facts are one-story men. Two-story men compare, reason, generalize, using the labors of fact collectors as well as their own. Three-story men idealize, imagine, predict—their best illumination comes from above, through the skylight.

—Oliver Wendell Holmes

From Bellanca and Fogarty (2003). *Blueprints for Achievement in the Cooperative Classroom.* Glenview, IL: SkyLight Professional Development. Used with permission by LessonLab, Glenview, IL.

EXAMPLES

PRIMARY

MATCHING QUESTIONS

Social Studies Test on Southeastern United States

Directions: (3 points each) Fill in the letter from Column B that the phrase in Column A is describing.

Column A	Column B
C 1. Changing crops from one year to another.	A. Cotton
G 2. Separated cotton seeds from cotton.	B. Tobacco
K 3. Someone who visits a place for pleasure.	C. Crop Rotation
A 4. Once referred to as "white gold."	D. Service Jobs
E 5. Biggest farms in Southeast.	E. Plantations
B 6. First cash crop.	F. Erosion
I 7. Crops grown to earn money.	G. Cotton Gin
D 8. Jobs in which people are served in some way.	H. Slave Labor
	I. Cash Crops
	J. Ranches
	K. Tourist

(Courtesy of Nancy Minske, Wheeling, Illinois.)

MIDDLE SCHOOL

GRAPHIC ORGANIZER

History

Directions: Complete the mind map on the Middle Ages by filling in the main components in the big circles and the subpoints in the smaller circles (1 point per circle).

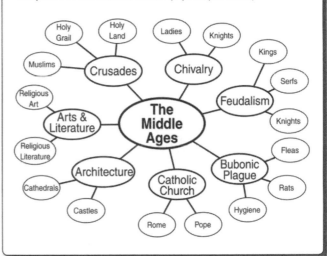

HIGH SCHOOL

TRUE-FALSE QUESTIONS

English

Directions: Please circle *true* next to the number if the statement is true; circle *false* if the statement is in any way false (2 points each). You will receive an additional 2 points if you rewrite the *false* statements to make them true.

(T) or F   1. Mark Twain wrote *Huckleberry Finn*.
Rewrite: _____

T or (F)   2. Tom Sawyer is the protagonist in *Huckleberry Finn*.
Rewrite: Tom Sawyer appears in *Huckleberry Finn*, but Huck Finn is the protagonist.

(T) or F   3. Mark Twain's real name is Samuel Clemens.
Rewrite: _____
_____

T or (F)   4. The runaway slave, Jim, hid on Hanibal Island after he left Aunt Polly.
Rewrite: He hid on Jackson Island. _____
_____

T or (F)   5. Mark Twain was a wealthy man all of his life.
Rewrite: Twain made a lot of money, but he went bankrupt by investing in bad businesses.

COLLEGE

ESSAY QUESTIONS

Science

Point Value: 20

Directions: Select *one* of the following topics for your essay question. Your essay will be evaluated on the following criteria:

- accuracy of information
- organization of information
- use of support statements
- clarity and effectiveness

Select *one* topic.

1. Predict what will happen if the ozone layer continues to deplete at its current rate.
2. Evaluate the effectiveness of our government's research and regulations regarding acid rain.
3. Speculate what will happen if a cure for AIDS is not found within five years.
4. Compare and contrast the bubonic plague to AIDS. You may draw a Venn diagram to help you organize your thoughts before you write.

Teacher-Made Tests

The Big Ten Checklist for Teacher-Made Tests

Test: _____ Date: _____

Grade Level/Class: _____

1. ____ I wrote my test *before* I taught the subject matter.

2. ____ I have listed my standards and benchmarks on the test.

3. ____ I have listed my grading scale on the test.

4. ____ I have varied the question types to include _____ types.

5. ____ I have provided point values for each section.

6. ____ I have included tasks to address the multiple intelligences and learning modalities of my students.

7. ____ I have given students some choice of questions.

8. ____ I have used all three levels of the Three-Story Intellect verbs in my questions.

9. ____ I have made allowances for students with special needs.

10. ____ I have made sure that all students have time to finish the test.

Signature: _____ Date: _____

ON YOUR OWN

Three-Story Intellect Verbs
Review

1. Analyze one of your own teacher-made tests. Classify the questions
    by marking them first, second, or third level according to the Three-Story
    Intellect (see p. 114). Tally the results.

    a. Number of first-story gathering questions.   _____

    b. Number of second-story processing questions.   _____

    c. Number of third-story applying questions.   _____

2. Analyze a chapter test from a textbook or any commercially prepared content
    test in terms of the guidelines used above. Tally the results.

    a. Number of first-story gathering questions.   _____

    b. Number of second-story processing questions.   _____

    c. Number of third-story applying questions.   _____

3. Compare and contrast the analysis of your original teacher-made test to your
    analysis of the commercially prepared test. Comment on your findings.

4. Construct an original teacher-made test to use with your students. Follow the
    guidelines discussed in this chapter and use The Big Ten Checklist for Teacher-Made
    Tests on page 116.

Teacher-Made Tests

 ## Teacher-Made Tests
3–2–1 Reflection

List *three* things you have learned about teacher-made tests.

3

1. _____

2. _____

3. _____

List *two* things you would like to try on your next teacher-made test.

2

1. _____

2. _____

List *one* comment you have about teacher-made tests.

1

_____

_____

LEARNING LOGS AND JOURNALS

CHAPTER 7

"We do not write and read primarily in order to ensure that this nation's employers can count on a competent, competitive work force. We write and read in order to know each other's responses, to connect ourselves more fully with the human world, and to strengthen the habit of truth-telling in our midst."

—DeMOTT, 1990, P. 6

Learning Logs and Journals

What Are Learning Logs and Journals?

Learning logs and reflective journals have been used by teachers as formative or ongoing assessment tools for years, but mostly by teachers of middle and high school English. Logs and journals are, however, beginning to play an even broader role in today's reflective classrooms with teachers in all content areas and grade levels.

Logs can consist of short, objective entries that contain mathematical problem-solving entries, observations of science experiments, questions about the lecture or readings, lists of outside readings, homework assignments, or anything that lends itself to keeping records. The responses in these logs are usually brief, factual, and impersonal.

Journals help students make connections between what is really important to them, the curriculum, and the world.

Journals, on the other hand, are usually written in narrative form, are subjective, and deal more with feelings, opinions, or personal experiences. Journal entries are usually more descriptive, longer, open ended, and more free flowing than logs. They are often used to respond to pieces of literature, describe events, comment on reactions to events, reflect on personal experiences and feelings, and connect what is being studied in one class with another class or with life outside the classroom. Csikszentmihalyi (as cited in Scherer, 2002) believes that journal writing can be therapy where students take charge of their learning and behavior. Journals help students make connections between what is really important to them, the curriculum, and the world. Educators must "nurture and cultivate that connection" (p. 17). The Venn diagram below shows similarities and differences between learning logs and journals.

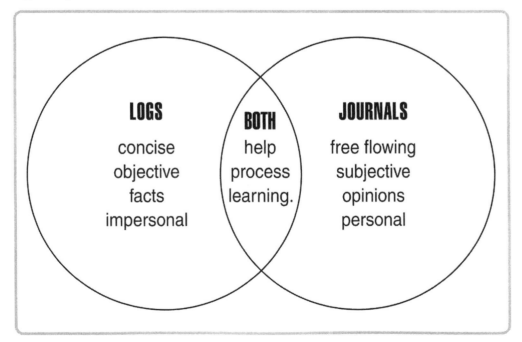

Research by Goodlad (1984) reveals that teachers at the high school level tend to lecture about 88 percent of the time. Students at all levels have attention spans from ten to fifteen minutes—on good days. Therefore, not only are students "turning off" the lecture, but they are also not retaining much of what is being said. Jensen (1998) states, "Teachers need to keep attentional demands to short bursts of no longer than the age of their learners in minutes. For a first grader, that's about 6 consecutive minutes; for a high schooler, student, that's up to 15 minutes" (p. 43).

Since it is important for students to interact with the teacher, the textbook, and each other, teachers often use logs and journals to help students process information during lectures. Teachers can give direct instruction in chunks of ten- to fifteen-minute segments, and then ask students to write down key ideas, questions, connections, or reflections. The students can use this time to think about the material, clarify confusion, discuss key ideas with group members, and process the information before the teacher moves on to the next segment of direct instruction. The following is an example of such a reflective lesson log technique.

Using a Reflective Lesson Log

1. The teacher presents information to the class. (10–15 minute chunks)
2. Students spend time writing in their reflective lesson log using the format shown below. (five minutes).

REFLECTIVE LESSON LOG

Name: _____ Topic: _____ Date: _____

Key ideas from this discussion: _____

_____

Connections I can make with other ideas: _____

_____

Questions I still have: _____

_____

_____

Learning Logs and Journals

3. Students then share their logs with a partner or group members. They discuss the key ideas with other students and see if they can answer each other's questions. (five minutes)
4. The teacher conducts a brief discussion with the whole class to see if anyone still has questions that were not answered or clarified by group members. The class then discusses the connections students made with the information to other subject areas or life experiences. (five minutes)
5. The teacher continues with the next chunk of direct instruction. The cycle repeats if there is time, or students complete logs for homework. Students discuss logs the following day as a review and to clarify any confusion they may have about their homework or yesterday's lesson. (ten minutes)

The advantages of structuring lessons to include the use of a reflective lesson log include the following:

1. Students retain key ideas.
2. Students' writing skills improve.
3. Students with special needs have more time to process information.
4. Interaction among students increases.
5. Students can study logs for quizzes and tests.
6. Learning logs can be included in portfolios.
7. Teachers can assign grades for selected logs or "log books" (daily grades or weekly grades).
8. Students who are absent can get logs from friends to keep up with work they missed.
9. Teachers can ascertain during the lesson if there is confusion or misunderstandings about information.
10. Students connect ideas they learn to real life.

Jensen (1998) recommends that teachers spend 55 to 80 percent of their time allowing students to process information. If teachers do not spend the time to allow students to process information, they may have to spend time re-teaching the information if students don't get it.

Why Should We Use Learning Logs and Journals?

Research by Brownlie, Close, and Wingren (1988); Jeroski, Brownlie, and Kaser (1990a); Barell (1992); and Costa, Bellanca, and Fogarty (1992a) recommends using logs and journals on a regular basis in the following ways:

1. *Record* key ideas from a lecture, movie, presentation, field trip, or reading assignment.
2. *Predict* what will happen next in a story, movie, or experiment; with the weather; or in school, national, or world events.
3. *List* questions.
4. *Summarize* the main ideas of a book, movie, lecture, or reading.
5. *Reflect* on the information presented.
6. *Connect* the ideas presented to other subject areas or to the students' personal lives.
7. *Monitor* change in an experiment or event over time.
8. *Respond* to questions posed by the teacher or other students.
9. *Brainstorm* ideas about potential projects, papers, or presentations.
10. *Identify* problems.
11. *Record* problem-solving techniques.
12. *Track* the number of problems solved, books read, or homework assignments completed.

Research recommends using logs and journals on a regular basis.

Brownlie, Close, and Wingren (1990) and Fogarty and Bellanca (1987) identify certain prompts or lead-ins that promote thinking at higher levels. Brownlie et al., suggest teachers use prompts at the beginning, middle, and end of a lesson, and to comment on the group process.

Some examples of prompts or lead-ins are:

At beginning of lesson
- What questions do you have from yesterday?
- Write two important points from yesterday's lesson.

In middle of lesson
- What do you want to know more about?
- How is this like something else?
- Is this easy or hard for you? Explain why.

Learning Logs and Journals

At the end of lesson
- Something I heard that surprised me was . . .
- How will you use this outside of class?

About the group process
- I helped move my group's thinking forward because . . .
- The group helped my thinking because . . .
- An example of collaboration today was . . .

Fogarty and Bellanca (1987) suggest lead-ins for logging that encourage responses that reflect analysis, synthesis, and evaluation. Examples of log stems include:

- One thing I'm excited about is _____ because . . .
- I hate it when _____ because . . .
- This is like a movie I saw _____ because . . .

Responding to new ideas in log or journal entries helps students process the information and reflect on their learnings.

Learning logs and journals are usually considered formative methods of assessment that can be assigned numerical or letter grades or point values.

How Should We Assess Learning Logs and Journals?

Learning logs and journals are usually considered formative methods of assessment that can be assigned numerical or letter grades or point values. The following methods of assessment may be helpful:

1. Jeroski, Brownlie, and Kaser (1990b) developed indicators to describe the depth and personalization of students' responses to their readings. They scored sixth grade students' responses to a poem using the following criteria: powerful, competent, partial, and undeveloped.

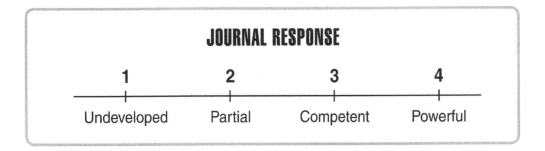

JOURNAL RESPONSE

1	2	3	4
Undeveloped	Partial	Competent	Powerful

2. Another way to assess journal responses is by the level of thoughtfulness: no evidence, little evidence, some evidence, and strong evidence.

JOURNAL RESPONSE

No Evidence of Thoughtfulness 1	Little Evidence of Thoughtfulness 2	Some Evidence of Thoughtfulness 3	Strong Evidence of Thoughtfulness 4
• No response	• Response only • Not supported by specific examples	• Response • Supported by specific examples	• Response • Supported by specific examples • Supported by personal reflections

3. Teachers can assign point values for logs or journals:

   20 points for completing all logs or journals
   10 points for completing all logs or journals on time
   15 points for originality of ideas
   15 points for evidence of higher-order thinking
   15 points for making connections to other subject areas
   20 points for personal examples
   <u>15 points for personal reflections or insights</u>

   100 total points for log and journal assignments

Learning Logs and Journals

4. Sample criteria and indicators that can be used to assess logs and journals on a checklist or rubric include the following:

- descriptive words
- use of examples
- length of response
- use of similes or metaphors
- dialogue
- connections to other subjects
- thoughtfulness
- originality
- creativity

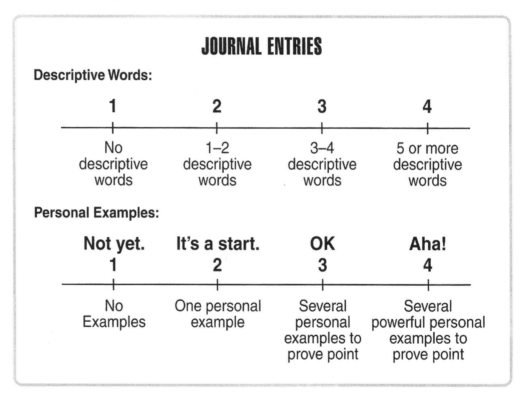

JOURNAL ENTRIES

Descriptive Words:

1	2	3	4
No descriptive words	1–2 descriptive words	3–4 descriptive words	5 or more descriptive words

Personal Examples:

Not yet. 1	It's a start. 2	OK 3	Aha! 4
No Examples	One personal example	Several personal examples to prove point	Several powerful personal examples to prove point

5. Students can turn in journals on a periodic basis for feedback and/or a grade. The grade can be based on the number of entries, the quality of entries (based on predetermined criteria), or a combination of quantity and quality.
6. Students can share journal entries with a buddy or a cooperative group. Peers may provide both oral and written feedback based on predetermined criteria.
7. Students may complete a self-assessment of their journal entries based on predetermined criteria provided in a checklist or a rubric, such as the one shown on page 127.

PRIMARY

JOURNAL WRITING

Standard: Use correct grammar, spelling, punctuation, capitalization, and sentence structure.

Early Elementary Benchmark: Write passages with correct grammar, spelling, punctuation, and sentence structure.

Scale: Criteria:	1 Back to the Drawing Board	2 School Newspaper	3 National Magazine	4 Pulitzer Prize for Writing
Correct grammar	5 or more errors	3–4 errors	1–2 errors	Flawless
Spelling	5 or more errors	3–4 errors	1–2 errors	Perfect
Punctuation	5 or more errors	3–4 errors	1–2 errors	All Correct
Capitalization	5 or more errors	3–4 errors	1–2 errors	Exceeds Standards
Sentence structure	5 or more errors	3–4 errors	1–2 errors	Beyond Expectations!

All teachers need to provide more opportunities for students to process what they have learned.

8. Students and teachers may select a few of the journal entries to be rewritten and turned in for a grade or be placed in the final portfolio.
9. Students and teachers could create a visual rubric that correlates to standards and benchmarks and can be used for self-assessment.

Recent brain research is providing educators with new information about how students learn. The evidence suggests that all teachers—not just English teachers—need to provide more opportunities for students to process what they have learned and to reflect on how that learning affects their lives. Keeping logs and journals are two self-assessment strategies that reinforce reflective teaching and learning by helping students construct knowledge for themselves.

Learning Logs and Journals

PRIMARY

GEOMETRY LOG

Picture of Shape	Word	Definition	Real Objects that Have the Shape	Describe When and Where You Might Need to Use this Shape
		Octagon		
		Triangle		
		Five Sides		
		Rectangle		
			Baseball Diamond	
		Four Sides – two short – two long		

What jobs or careers require a knowledge of geometry? Explain.

(Courtesy of Lynette Russell, Northbrook, Illinois.)

MIDDLE SCHOOL

DOUBLE-ENTRY JOURNAL

Name: Juan   **Date:** September 3

Grade: 7

Topic: Home Economics

Initial Observation (Sept. 3)	Upon Reflection (Sept. 15)
I think it's really stupid that boys have to take home economics. Why should I have to learn to sew and cook? I don't plan on ever doing it. I'd rather take a computer or another physical education course. There's only five guys in this class. I'm going to go to my counselor during homeroom tomorrow and try to get out of here!	Well, the counselor said all the sections of the computer were full, so I'm stuck in here for the quarter. I still don't believe it but my Apple Brown Betty was pretty good! I guess it wouldn't hurt to learn a few cooking tricks. Maybe this won't be so bad. Besides, I've met a lot of cool girls!

HIGH SCHOOL

JOURNAL STEMS

Student: Penny   **Date:** Sept. 10

Topic: Social Studies   **Grade:** 10

Select one of the following stem statements to use in your journal entry:

Stem Statements

A. The best part about . . .   E. How . . .

B. An interesting part is . . .   F. Why . . .

C. I predict . . .   G. A connecting idea is . . .

D. I wonder . . .   H. I believe . . .

Journal Entry:

I predict that P.E. classes will be required for all students through 12th grade. Right now it is an elective for 10th grade, but one of the most important things in life is staying healthy. Exercise is a life skill that is as important as English or math.

COLLEGE

PROBLEM-SOLVING LOG

Name: Jeff   **Date:** September 10

Class: Comp 101

My problem is . . .

1. I'm stuck on . . .
   choosing a thesis statement for my research paper.

2. The best way to think about this is . . .
   writing a statement that states my opinion.

3. Something that is similar to this problem is . . .
   my senior year research paper.

4. A question I still have is . . .
   Do I have three major subpoints for the thesis?

5. One solution I think could work is . . .
   doing some preliminary research.

6. I need help with . . .
   writing the statement so it is parallel.

ON YOUR OWN

3–2–1 Reflective Log

Name: _____   **Date:** _____

Topic: _____   **Standard:** _____

3 key ideas from this chapter:

a.

b.

c.

2 connections I can make with other ideas:

a.

b.

1 question I still have:

Question: _____

Learning Logs and Journals

Journal Stems

1. Create some original stem statements that would motivate your students to write in their logs or journals.

Example: My worst nightmare is . . .   My friends would never believe that . . .

Journal Stem Statements

*   _____   *   _____

*   _____   *   _____

*   _____   *   _____

2. Response journals require students to respond to a particular stimulus like a field trip, an assembly speaker, or a newspaper article. List some activities that your students could respond to in a journal.

Response Journal Topics

_____   _____

_____   _____

_____   _____

_____   _____

_____   _____

Learning Logs and Journals

List two ideas for using learning logs and two ideas for using journals with your students.

Logs

1. _____

_____

_____

2. _____

_____

_____

Journals

1. _____

_____

_____

2. _____

_____

_____

METACOGNITIVE REFLECTION

CHAPTER 8

"Basically, metacognition means that, when confronted with a dilemma or some obstacle, humans draw on their mental resources to plan a course of action, monitor that strategy while executing it, then reflect on the strategy to evaluate its productiveness in terms of the outcomes it was intended to achieve."

—COSTA, IN HYERLE, 1996, P. 23

Metacognitive Reflection

What Is Metacognitive Reflection?

Swartz and Perkins define metacognition as "becoming aware of your thought processes in order to then control them when appropriate" (as cited in Barell, 1992, p. 258). Barell (1992) states that researchers and practitioners usually focus primarily on the cognitive when discussing metacognition because that is part of the definition: metacognitive is *along* or *beyond* one's cognitive operations. But Barell argues that feelings, attitudes, and dispositions play a vital role in metacognition since "*thinking* involves not only cognitive operations but the dispositions to engage in them when and where appropriate" (p. 259). He also talks about the importance of asking students to think about their own thinking. "'Tell me how you arrived at that' is the process of raising their consciousness and therefore improving their control over how they approach tasks" (p. 99).

Metacognitive reflections allow students to manage and assess their own thinking strategies.

Metacognitive reflections allow students to manage and assess their own thinking strategies. "Metacognition involves the monitoring and control of attitudes, such as students' beliefs about themselves, the value of persistence, the nature of work, and their personal responsibility in accomplishing a goal" (Fusco and Fountain, 1992, p. 240). These attitudes are essential components in all tasks—academic and nonacademic.

Teachers need to introduce strategies that promote metacognition. Moreover, students need to self-reflect regularly so they can become adept at monitoring, assessing, and improving their own performances and their own thinking.

One of the key pieces in the portrait of a student for the twenty-first century involves self-assessment. In teachers' attempt to cover the content, teach the textbook, and prepare students for the test, they often neglect the critical piece that allows everyone to step back and reflect on what we did well, what we would do differently, and whether or not we need help. Individual students, cooperative groups, and teachers need to take the time to process what they have done and to reflect on their own learning. The more connections that students can make between past learning and new learning, the more likely they are to make sense of the meaning and retain the learning.

Why Should We Use Metacognitive Reflection?

Perkins and Salomon (1992) and Fogarty, Perkins, and Barell (1992) all describe the critical relationships between metacognition and transfer. "In order to transfer knowledge or skills from one situation to another, we must be aware of them; metacognitive strategies are designed to help students become more aware" (Barell, 1992, p. 259). Moye (1997) explains that, in essence, transfer and mastery are synonymous. Metacognition leads to transfer.

Fogarty, Perkins, and Barell (1992) define transfer as "learning something in one context and applying it in another" (p. ix). They give examples of how people can learn to drive a car (the first context), and then later, when they have to rent a small truck, they can drive it fairly well (the second context). Or when one learns a foreign language such as French, some of the vocabulary may carry over to Italian.

Transfer of knowledge plays a key role in metacognition.

Transfer

Educators used to think that students will automatically take what teachers teach and apply or transfer it to other places or areas. Yet, students often do not connect what they learn in English class to social studies class, or what they learn in math class to a mathematical problem they encounter at work or in life. Transfer of knowledge plays a key role in metacognition. An example of a transfer journal is on p. 142.

It is evident that transfer does not happen automatically unless teachers teach for it. Journals, thoughtful questioning, goal setting, problem-based learning, and self-assessments can help make students become more aware of their thought processes and, therefore, more able to transfer those strategies to real-life situations.

Transfer is an integral component of the learning process. Every day teachers refer to past learning to make new learning more understandable and meaningful. Students are expected to transfer the knowledge and skills they learn in school to the context of everyday life. Sousa (2001, p. 139) states, "It is almost axiomatic that the more information students can transfer from their schooling to the context of everyday life, the greater the probability that they will be good communicators, informed citizens, critical thinkers, and successful problem solvers." The more connections students can make between past learning and new learning, the more likely they are to make sense of the meaning and retain the learning.

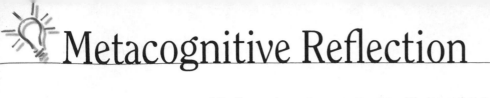

Metacognitive Reflection

"Ordinary learning contrasts with transfer. In ordinary learning, we just do more of the same thing in the same situations. . . . Real transfer happens when people carry over something they learned in one context to a 'significantly different' context" (Fogarty, Perkins, and Barell, 1992, p. ix). Fogarty et al. (1992) use the graphic on page 137 to illustrate the situational dispositions for transfer. They use six birds to represent the different models.

Successful transfer is enhanced when educators use thematic units and an integrated curriculum. Sousa (2001) believes that an integrated approach to learning helps students see the commonalities among diverse topics and reinforces understanding and meaning for future applications.

Situational Dispositions for Transfer

Model	Illustration	Transfer Disposition	Looks Like	Sounds Like
Ollie the Head-in-the-Sand Ostrich		**Overlooks**	Persists in writing in manuscript form rather than cursive. (New skill overlooked or avoided.)	*"I get it right on the dittos, but I forget to use punctuation when I write an essay."* (Not applying mechanical learning.)
Dan the Drilling Woodpecker		**Duplicates**	Plagiarism is the most obvious student artifact of duplication. (Unable to synthesize in own words.)	*"Mine is not to question why—just invert and multiply* (when dividing fractions). (No understanding of what he or she is doing.)
Laura the Look-Alike Penguin		**Replicates**	"Bed to Bed" or narrative style. "He got up. He did this. He went to bed." Or "He was born. He did this. He died." (Student portfolio of work never varies.)	*"Paragraphing means I must have three 'indents' per page."* (Tailors into own story or essay, but paragraphs inappropriately.)
Jonathan Livingston Seagull		**Integrates**	Student writing essay incorporates newly learned French words. (Applying: weaving old and new.)	*"I always try to guess (predict) what's going to happen next on T.V. shows."* (Connects to prior knowledge and experience; relates what's learned to personal experience.)
Cathy the Carrier Pigeon		**Maps**	Graphs information for a social studies report with the help of the math teacher to actually design the graphs. (Connecting to another.)	From a parent: *"Tina suggested we brainstorm our vacation ideas and rank them to help us decide."* (Carries new skills into life situations.)
Samantha the Soaring Eagle		**Innovates**	After studying flow charts for computer class, student constructs a Rube Goldberg-type invention. (Innovates; diverges; goes beyond and creates novelty.)	*"I took the idea of the Mr. Potato Head and created a mix-and-match grid of ideas for our Earth Day project."* (Generalizes ideas from experience and transfers creatively.)

From *The Mindful School: How to Teach for Transfer* by Fogarty, Perkins, and Barell. Copyright ©1992 by IRI/Skylight Publishing. Reprinted with permission of LessonLab, Glenview, IL.

Metacognitive Reflection

How Should We Use Metacognitive Reflection?

Logs and Journals

Teachers can use logs and journals as metacognitive strategies by assessing the reflectiveness of the students' responses, the evidence of transfer to other classes or life outside school, and the students' abilities to plan, monitor, and evaluate their own work.

Teachers can use logs and journals as metacognitive strategies.

Self-Assessment Questions

Fogarty and Bellanca (1987) suggest a series of questions called Mrs. Potter's Questions to help individuals and groups process and reflect on their individual work or their group work.

MRS. POTTER'S QUESTIONS

1. What were you expected to do?
2. In this assignment, what did you do well?
3. If you had to do this task over, what would you do differently?
4. What help do you need from me?

Stiggins (2002, p. 762) believes that teachers need to engage students in regular self-assessment with the standards held constant so that "students can watch themselves grow over time and thus feel in charge of their own success."

KWL

This strategy, devised by Donna Ogle (1986), helps students approach a topic by asking two initial questions: (1) What do we already *know* about this topic and (2) *What* would we like to find out? At the end of the unit, the students complete the last column that stresses metacognition; and (3) What have we *learned* about this topic? The KWL is a graphic organizer that monitors prior knowledge, students' interests, and application and evaluation. (See the example of KWL on page 141.)

Wait Time

Wait time is the period of silence after the teacher poses a question before he or she calls on the first student for a response. When Rowe (1974) first conducted research, she found that high school teachers had an average wait time of just over one second. Elementary teachers waited an average of three seconds. Slower retrievers, many of whom may know the correct answer, do not have enough time to locate the answer in long-term memory storage and retrieve it into working memory. Sousa (2001, p. 128) feels that "as soon as the teacher calls on the first student, the remaining students stop the retrieval process and lose the opportunity to relearn the information."

Rowe (as cited in Sousa, 2001) found that if teachers extended the wait time to at least five seconds or more, the length and quality of student responses increased, there was greater participation by slower learners, students used more evidence to support inferences, and there were more higher-order responses.

PMI

The metacognitive strategy developed by de Bono (1992) helps students evaluate their learning by asking them to write either individually or in groups, what were the *pluses* (P); what were the *minuses* (M); and what was *intriguing* or *interesting* (I) about the topic. The strategy helps students become independent thinkers and critical self-evaluators of their learning. This strategy is usually implemented at the end of an assignment or unit as a means to evaluate its effectiveness. (See example PMI on page 141.)

Group Processing

Students need to reflect on their participation in group work and continually ask themselves and their fellow group members what they can do to improve their social skills. An example of a group processing strategy using a car race metaphor can be found on page 143.

Final Thoughts

Teachers in the twenty-first century need to possess a content knowledge base that they will transfer to their students. But knowledge base alone is not enough. Metacognitive strategies can help teachers possess a *pedagogical content knowledge,* a knowledge that Shulman (1988, p. 9) calls "a knowledge

Students need to reflect on their participation in group work.

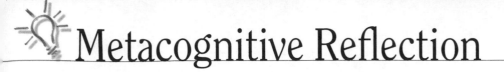

of the most useful forms of representation of ideas, the most powerful analogies, illustrations, examples, explanations, and demonstrations— in a word, the ways of representing and formulating the subject that makes it comprehensible to others."

Metacognitive strategies help teachers gain psychological insight into students that multiple-choice objective tests cannot provide. In John Dewey's "Pedagogic Creed," written in 1897, he said, "Education, therefore, must begin with a psychological insight into the child's capacities, interests, and habits. It must be controlled at every point by reference to these same considerations" (in Eisner, 1994, p. vi). Metacognitive and transfer strategies help provide insights into the student's mind.

PRIMARY

KWL

Name: Juan **Date:** Sept. 15
Topic: Middle Ages – 6th grade

What I *Know* about topic	What I *Want* to Find Out	What I *Learned*
The knights went on crusades.	Why did knights go on crusades?	Knights went on Crusades to get back the Holy Land
People died from the plague.	Did the rats cause the plague?	Fleas from the rats spread germs.
Castles were surrounded by moats.	Why did castles have moats around them?	Moats were used for sewage and protection.

Note: The KWL strategy was developed by Donna Ogle (1986).

MIDDLE SCHOOL

PMI

Write how you feel about the topic: Using Portfolios

Plus (+)	Minus (–)	Interesting (?)
It's fun to see my work over a whole year.	I have to be organized.	Someday I'll look back and laugh.
I see growth.	I have to reflect on all I do.	Even my grandmother wants to see it.
It shows what I want to work on more.	I could lose it.	My brother took his when he went to a job interview.
My parents like to see all the stuff.	I have to decide what to put in it.	I got to put a video of our group skit in.
I have my artwork and pictures of my projects.	I don't like to see other kids who have good ones.	It's better than tests!
I'll keep it in my basement until I graduate.	I have to think!	Now I can remember what I learned.

Note: The PMI strategy was developed by Edward deBono (1992).

HIGH SCHOOL

REFLECTION

Name: Josh **Date:** October 6
Course: Science – 9th grade **Topic:** AIDS

Circle One: (Lecture) Discussion Video Written material

1. Key Ideas:
   - It's spreading fast.
   - No cure
   - Kids can get it from transfusions.
2. Questions I have:
   - Can you get it by kissing?
   - Is the blood supply safe?
3. Connections I can make with other subjects: social studies
   - AIDS reminds me of the Black Death during the Middle Ages.
4. How I can apply these ideas to my own life:
   - I better find out if you can get it by kissing—I need to learn more.
5. My insights or reflections from these ideas:
   - I really don't know that much about AIDS. We'll see the video tomorrow. Maybe I'll learn more.

COLLEGE

SELF-ASSESSMENT

Name: Cedric **Date:** Jan. 7
Assignment: Speech 101

1. What were you supposed to do?
   Give a speech on my favorite hobby.
2. What was your favorite part?
   Bringing my baseball card collection to college—no one in my class has ever seen it before.
3. What was your least favorite part? Why?
   Having to write an outline—my mind doesn't think in roman numerals.
4. If you did this task over, what would you do differently? Why?
   Get a better ending—I just stopped! I should have thrown a baseball or something dramatic.
5. What grade do you think you deserve and why?
   B—People remember the last thing you say, and my last thing wasn't too memorable.
6. What new goal can you set for yourself?
   Practice a better ending—some of the other speeches had quotes or jokes—mind had a fact—Blah!

Metacognitive Reflection

Transfer Journal

Name: _____ Class/Course: _____ Date: _____

Idea	Interpretation	Application
What's the Big Idea? (Copy phrase or sentence exactly)	**What does it mean?** (Write in your own words)	**How can you apply or transfer the idea to another subject or your life?**
Example: Vietnam became President Johnson's *Achilles' heel*.	Soft spot, weakness—In mythology Achilles was dipped in the River Styx to make him invincible. His mother held him by the heel, which wasn't protected. He was later killed when someone shot him in the heel.	I can say that when I diet, chocolate is my *Achilles' heel*—my weak spot—my downfall. In the book *A Separate Peace*, Gene's *Achilles' heel* (downfall) was jealousy. He envied Finny, and his envy caused Finny's death.

Signed: _____ Date: _____

Group Processing: How Did We Do?

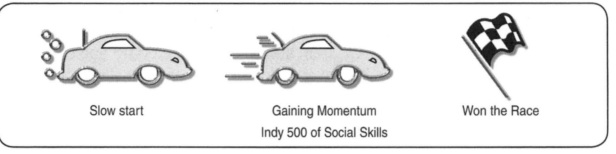

Slow start

Gaining Momentum
Indy 500 of Social Skills

Won the Race

1. How did we stay on task?

Slow start

Gaining Momentum
Indy 500 of Social Skills

Won the Race

2. How did we listen to each other?

Slow start

Gaining Momentum
Indy 500 of Social Skills

Won the Race

3. How did we encourage each other?

Slow start

Gaining Momentum
Indy 500 of Social Skills

Won the Race

4. What do we need to work on next time?

5. How do we want to celebrate our successes?

Adapted from Burke, K., *What to Do with the Kid Who . . .: Developing Cooperation, Self-Discipline, and Responsibility in the Classroom* (p. 115). © 2000 by SkyLight Professional Development. Reprinted with permission of LessonLab, Glenview, IL.

Metacognitive Reflection

Wraparound

The wraparound is an effective reflective strategy that teachers can use in the middle or at the end of a lesson to find out how students feel and what they remember about a lesson. Write a few stem statements on the board and divide the room so that students know what stem question they will answer. Give enough wait time to allow everyone time to reflect. Go around the room and call on each student to complete the stem statement assigned, or let the students select any one to complete.

Sample Wraparound Stems

One idea I learned today is . . .

The fact that really surprised me is . . .

One thing I'll remember 25 years from now is . . .

One idea I would like to learn more about is . . .

Create your own wraparound stems to use with your class.

Wraparound Stems

Stem: _____

Stem: _____

Stem: _____

Stem: _____

Ask your students to help create their own stems.

Metacognitive Reflection

Select two strategies from the ones introduced in this chapter (logs and journals, Mrs. Potter's Questions, KWL, wait time, PMI, group processing, wraparound) and describe how you plan to use them with your students.

Strategy One

_____

_____

_____

_____

_____

_____

_____

Strategy Two

_____

_____

_____

_____

_____

_____

_____

_____

OBSERVATION CHECKLISTS

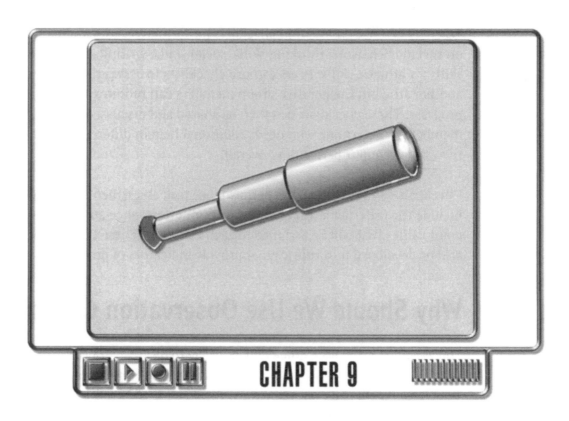

CHAPTER 9

"As inquirers, teachers are always observing and gathering information about their students. This can be done informally through class discussions or more formally through such things as written assignments, group projects, plays, or classroom assessments."

—LANGER, COLTON & GOFF, 2003, P. 33

Observation Checklists

What Are Observation Checklists?

The observation checklist is a strategy to monitor specific skills, behaviors, or dispositions of individual students or all of the students in the class. It is also a record-keeping device for teachers to use to keep track of who has mastered the targeted skills and who still needs help. Effective observation checklists include the student's name, space for four to five targeted areas, a code or rating to determine to what degree the student has or has not demonstrated the skill (+ = frequently; √ = sometimes; o = not yet!), and a space for comments or anecdotal notes. Some teachers find it useful to date the occurrences so they can see developmental growth or use the checklists for student and parent conferences.

The checklist provides a quick and easy way to observe and record skills, criteria, and behaviors.

Teachers can use observation checklists for formative assessments by focusing on specific behaviors, thinking skills, social skills, writing skills, speaking skills, or athletic skills. Peers can use checklists to assess the progress of another student. Cooperative group members can monitor the entire group's progress. These checklists can then be shared and discussed among group members to determine who needs additional help in different areas and how the whole group is performing overall.

Checklists can also be used as performance task assessment lists. These lists include the criteria for a specific project or performance and sometimes the point values that will be assigned to each criterion. These types of lists can also be developed into rubrics that provide indicators of quality.

Why Should We Use Observation Checklists?

The checklist provides a quick and easy way to observe and record many of the skills, criteria, and behaviors prior to the final test or summative evaluation. Too often, teachers do not realize a student needs help until it is too late. Checklists show teachers and students the areas of concern early enough to be able to help students before they fail the test or the unit. They also provide teachers the opportunity to "change gears" in a classroom if a large percentage of the students are not doing well. Checklists provide formative assessments of students' learning and help teachers monitor whether or not students are on track to meet the standards.

Guskey (2003) recommends creating checklists that list the teacher's clear criteria for judging students' performances. The checklists contain specific criteria aligned with instructional strategies and, ideally, with state or district standards. Students see these assessments as fair and teachers use them to provide immediate feedback and to focus on trouble spots for an individual student, a small group of students, or the whole class. "The best classroom assessments also serve as meaningful sources of information for teachers, helping them identify what they taught well and what they need to work on" (p. 8).

Costa (1991) recommends that characteristics of intelligent behavior such as persistence, listening, flexibility in thinking, metacognition, and checking for accuracy as well as precision can be taught and observed by students, parents, and teachers. Observation checklists are tools to use to check whether or not the student can demonstrate the skill or attribute being measured. Observation checklists also focus on observable performances or criteria that are often more meaningful or authentic than paper-and-pencil tests. By focusing on two or three concrete skills or criteria, teachers and students can monitor growth or pinpoint a need for improvement more easily.

Observation checklists focus on observable performances or criteria that are often more meaningful or authentic than paper-and-pencil tests.

Observation is one of the most effective tools to find out what children can do and what their learning needs are. In a resource guide for parents and teachers that discusses how to assess the progress of primary-age children, the Ministry of Education in British Columbia (1991a) recommends that teachers watch children throughout the year and "record observations of children in action and review them on a regular basis to discover patterns, assess progress, and make plans to help children continue their learning" (p. 14). The Ministry recommends that teachers structure tasks to develop a base of information about each child and use the checklist to chart progress over time.

Teachers and parents can observe children in a variety of settings:

- classrooms
- playground
- field trips
- hallways
- gym

- individually
- in groups (pairs, small or large groups)
- with younger children
- with older children
- with adults

Observation Checklists

It is possible to observe children performing a variety of tasks:

- reading
- writing
- computing
- problem solving
- listening
- sorting
- playing music
- dramatizing

- constructing
- talking
- map making
- classifying
- painting
- typing
- miming
- socializing

- dancing
- playing
- building
- drawing
- singing
- working
- graphing
- word processing

(Ministry of Education, Province of British Columbia, 1991b, p. 14)

Students should be trained in what the skill looks like and sounds like if they are going to be asked to observe their peers or perform a self-assessment.

By observing children and charting their progress on notecards, observation checklists, sticky notes, or portfolios, teachers can learn about students' learning styles, learning needs, attitudes, initiative, likes and dislikes, and need for assistance (Ministry, 1991a).

How Should We Use Observation Checklists?

Each teacher can determine which specific areas to include in the observation checklist and then make sure the students are aware of the areas that will be observed. Students should be trained in what the skill looks like and sounds like if they are going to be asked to observe their peers or perform a self-assessment. It is imperative that the skills and processes being observed are modeled and taught to the students prior to the observations.

Individual Checklists

For example, if students are going to be observed on persistence, they should work with the teacher to list observable indicators of persistence on an individual checklist. A model checklist for persistence is shown on the following page.

CRITERION: PERSISTENCE

Indicators:	Not Yet Observed	Sometimes Observed	Frequently Observed
1. Knows how to access information			
2. Tries several approaches			
3. Does not give up quickly			
4. Has patience			
5. Brainstorms alternative solutions			
6. Checks own work			

Developing Criteria

Guskey (2001) believes teachers need to classify grading criteria into three broad categories: product, process, and progress.

- **Product criteria** describe what students know and are able to do at a particular point in time. Teachers use product criteria to grade final products such as reports, projects, portfolios, and performances.
- **Process criteria** describe how students achieved the final product. Teachers consider student effort, class behavior, work habits, daily work, regular quizzes, homework, class participation, punctuality of assignments, or attendance.
- **Progress criteria** describe how much the students actually gain from their learning experiences. This might include learning gain, improvement grading, value-added grading, and educational growth. Progress criteria look at how far the students have come rather than where students are, allowing for a very individualized judgment of students' "learning potential" (pp. 21–22).

One of the first steps in creating an observation checklist is to develop specific indicators that describe the skills, actions, or behaviors that are expected in terms of a criterion. Students need concrete examples. Asking a student to be more attentive or more persistent is abstract. Listing specific behaviors or skills is concrete. It is sometimes developmentally appropriate to start with specifics on a checklist and then move to the abstract after students know the expectations. A checklist could be as simple as criteria with a 0 for not observed and a 1 for observed. A kindergarten skills checklist could consist of the following:

Observation Checklists

Observation checklists help make abstract behaviors more concrete.

KINDERGARTEN SKILLS CHECKLIST

Indicators:	Not Yet 0	Yes 1
1. Can write name		
2. Knows phone number		
3. Can write address		
4. Recognizes different colors		
5. Can count to 25		
6. Knows alphabet		
7. Speaks in complete sentences		
8. Knows directions to school		

T-Charts

Another way teachers can work with students to identify key characteristics or indicators of observable skills, attitudes, dispositions, behaviors, or processes is to develop a graphic organizer called a T-chart. A T-chart helps students understand what certain behaviors look like and sound like. As demonstrated in the example below, if a teacher is observing the social skill "encouragement," the entire class can complete a T-chart prior to the observation. It is often the conversations and discussions about the skill that generate understanding of the final T-chart product.

ENCOURAGEMENT

What does it look like?	What does it sound like?
1. Looking at the person who is talking	1. "I like that idea."
2. Nodding your head	2. "Tell me more."
3. Patting the person on the back	3. "What do you think?"
4. Using a sign like thumbs-up or high five	4. "Good job."
5. Applauding appropriately	5. "We really want your opinion."

See page 154 for another example of a T-chart developed as an accuracy checklist.

Most teachers find they have more success if they create a T-chart first, develop an observation checklist from key criteria on the T-chart second, and then develop a rubric to include indicators of quality. In general, observation checklists help make abstract behaviors more concrete for students and teachers and help make assessments more aligned with instruction.

EXAMPLES

PRIMARY

SOCIAL SKILLS CHECKLIST

ASSESSMENT OF SOCIAL SKILLS

Date: 10/21
Class: 3rd Grade
Teacher: Forbes

Ratings:
+ = Frequently
✔ = Sometimes
○ = Not Yet

Skill headings (diagonal): Listening, Using first names, Taking turns, Encouraging, Sharing

Who	Skill 1	Skill 2	Skill 3	Skill 4	Skill 5	Comments
1. Lois	✔	✔	○	✔	✔	
2. Connie	+	+	○	✔	+	Dropped in 2 areas
3. James	✔	✔	✔	✔	✔	
4. Juan	+	+	✔	+	+	
5. Beth	○	○	+	✔	✔	Improved in 2 areas
6. Michele	✔	✔	○	✔	✔	
7. John	✔	✔	○	✔	✔	
8. Charles	+	+	○	✔	+	
9. Mike	✔	✔	✔	✔	✔	Went from 5 0s to this in 2 months
10. Lana	+	+	✔	+	+	

Notes: Work with Lois on a regular basis. Change her seat and group.

MIDDLE SCHOOL

OBSERVATION CHECKLIST

Student: Denise   Class: Science   Date: 12/5
Type of Assignment: Work habits

☐ Teacher Date _____ Signed _____
☐ Peer   Date _____ Signed _____
☒ Self   Date 12/5   Signed Denise Smith

	Not Yet	Sometimes	Frequently
WORK HABITS			
• Gets work done on time			X
• Asks for help when needed		X	
• Takes initiative		X	
STUDY HABITS			
• Organizes work			X
• Takes good notes			X
• Uses time well			X
PERSISTENCE			
• Shows patience		X	
• Checks own work	X		
• Revises work		X	
• Does quality work			X
SOCIAL SKILLS			
• Works well with others		X	
• Listens to others		X	
• Helps others		X	

COMMENTS: I always get my work done on time, and I am really organized. I just need to check my own work and help my group work.

Future goal: I need to be more patient with my group and try to work with them more. I worry about my own grades, but I don't do enough to help group members achieve their goals.

HIGH SCHOOL

BASKETBALL SKILLS

Teacher: Ms. Moses   Class: 5th Period P.E.   Date: 11/22
Target Skill: Students will develop basketball skills and teamwork.

STUDENTS DEMONSTRATE THE FOLLOWING

Ratings:
+ = Frequently
✔ = Sometimes
○ = Not Yet

Skill headings (diagonal): Dribbling skills, Passing skills, Free throw skills, Team spirit, Sportsmanship

Names of Students						Comments
1. Toni	✔	+	○	○	✔	
2. Casey	+	+	○	✔	+	
3. James	✔	✔	○	✔	✔	
4. Juan	+	+	✔	+	+	Real potential
5. Beth	✔	✔	✔	✔	✔	
6. Michele	✔	✔	○	✔	✔	Practice free throws
7. Judy	+	○	✔	+	+	
8. Charles	○	○	+	✔	✔	Does not like team sports
9. Dave	✔	+	○	✔	+	
10. Lisa	+	+	✔	+	+	Excellent player

COLLEGE

WRITING CHECKLIST

Key:
+ = Good
✔ = OK
○ = Not Yet

☐ Teacher
☐ Peer
☒ Self

Student: Robin   Class: English 102
Paper: Teaching for transfer

	Date: 9/1	Date: 11/5	Date: 1/2
Usage			
1. Topic sentence	+	+	+
2. Complete sentences	+	+	+
3. Complex sentences	○	○	○
4. Wide vocabulary	○	✔	+
Mechanics			
5. Capitalization	+	+	+
6. Punctuation	✔	✔	✔
7. Spelling	○	✔	+
8. Grammar	✔	✔	+

Strengths: My topic sentences, sentence structure, and capitalization are good.

Not Yet: I need to write more complex sentences. Most of my sentences are simple.

Observation Checklists

T-Chart Graphic Organizer

The T-chart is a graphic organizer that helps teachers and students focus on the specific behaviors that can be observed.

SKILL: Intelligent behavior; checking for accuracy

What does it look like?	What does it sound like?
Using spell check Using a dictionary Checking sources Having a peer read material Proofreading carefully Reading aloud Using a calculator	"How do you spell *receive?* "Where is our grammar reference book?" "Give me the thesaurus." "Will you edit this for me?" "Let me check my figures again." "This is my third draft."

Select one criterion or skill from the Criteria for Checklists lists on page 155 and complete a T-chart with your class.

Criterion/Skill: _____

What does it look like?	What does it sound like?

ON YOUR OWN

Criteria for Checklists

WRITING

Grammar and Usage
Sentence structure
Subject-verb agreement
Comma splices
Plurals of nouns
Pronouns/agreement
Verb tenses
Use of adjectives
Use of adverbs
Fragments
Run-on sentences

Mechanics
Capitalization
Commas
Semicolons
Colons
Question marks
Apostrophes
Spelling

Organization
Outline
Introduction
Topic sentences
Support sentences
Transitions
Conclusion

Research Skills
Selection of topic
Review of literature
Working bibliography
Thesis statement
Outline
Paraphrasing
Documentation
Final bibliography
Proofreading

SPEAKING AND READING

Speaking Skills
Eye contact
Facial expression
Voice inflection
Enthusiasm
Organization
Use of facts
Visual aids
Movement
Persuasiveness
Body language
Gestures

Oral Reading
Pronunciation
Enunciation
Expression
Fluency

Study Skills
Prereading
Webs
Venn diagrams
KWL
Surveys
Q3K
Idea wrapping
Think-pair-share

Reading Readiness
Chooses to read during
    free time
Visits school library
Begins reading quickly
Talks about books

SOCIAL SKILLS

Formation of Groups
Forms groups quietly
Sits face to face
Makes eye contact
Uses first names
Shares materials
Follows role assignments

Support
Checks for understanding
Offers help
Asks the group for help
Encourages others
Energizes the group
Disagrees with the
    idea—not the person

Communication
Uses a low voice
Takes turns
Makes sure everyone speaks
Waits until speaker is finished
    before speaking

Conflict Resolution
Disagrees with the idea—not
    the person
Respects the opinion of
    others
Thinks for self
Explores different points of
    view
Negotiates and/or compro-
    mises
Reaches consensus

PROBLEM SOLVING

Critical Thinking
Analyzing bias
Attributing cause and
    effect
Classifying
Comparing
Contrasting
Decision making
Drawing conclusions
Evaluating
Inferring
Prioritizing
Sequencing
Solving analogies

Creative Thinking
Brainstorming
Generalizing
Hypothesizing
Inventing
Making analogies
Recognizing
    paradoxes
Personifying
Predicting
Problem solving

INTELLIGENT BEHAVIORS

Persistence
Listening
Flexibility in thinking

Metacognition
Checking for accuracy
Precision

Observation Checklists

Observation Checklist

Directions: Select the skills you want to observe and write them on the five slanted lines at the top of the numbered list.

Teacher: _____ Class: _____ Date: _____

Target Skills: _____

Ratings:
   + = Frequently
   ✔ = Sometimes
   ○ = Not Yet

Names of Students						Comments
1.						
2.						
3.						
4.						
5.						
6.						
7.						
8.						
9.						
10.						
11.						
12.						
13.						
14.						
15.						
16.						
17.						
18.						
19.						

ON YOUR OWN

Individual Observation Checklist

Directions: Select criteria you want to observe and list specific indicators that describe those criteria (see Middle School: Observation Checklist example on page 153).

Student: _____ Class: _____ Date: _____

Type of Assignment: _____

☐ Teacher Date _____ Signed _____

☐ Peer Date _____ Signed _____

☐ Self Date _____ Signed _____

	Not yet 0	Sometimes 1	Frequently 2

• _____	____	____	____
• _____	____	____	____
• _____	____	____	____

• _____	____	____	____
• _____	____	____	____
• _____	____	____	____

• _____	____	____	____
• _____	____	____	____
• _____	____	____	____

• _____	____	____	____
• _____	____	____	____
• _____	____	____	____

Comments: _____
_____
_____

EXAMPLE

Research Report Checklist

Before you submit the rough draft of your research report, please complete a self-evaluation of your work by checking the "Me" column. Ask a peer to check your work in the "Peer" column. I will check your work in the "Teacher" column.

Me	Peer	Organization	Teacher
_____	_____	1. Minimum of fifteen bibliography cards	_____
_____	_____	2. Minimum of twenty-five notecards	_____
_____	_____	3. Outline with at least five major points	_____
_____	_____	4. Final paper with eight to ten pages, typed and double-spaced	_____

Format

Me	Peer		Teacher
_____	_____	5. Thesis statement with three supporting ideas	_____
_____	_____	6. Ten quotations from experts	_____
_____	_____	7. No spelling and grammar errors	_____
_____	_____	8. All paragraphs contain topic sentences, three support sentences, and concluding sentence.	_____

Student signature _____

Peer signature _____ Date _____

EXAMPLE

Listening for Comprehension
(Grades 6–12, Intermediate Level)

Name: _____ Date: _____

Grade: _____ Teacher: _____

Standards:

6–12.1—Comprehends high-frequency words and basic phrases, produces learned words and phrases, and uses appropriate gestures to communicate.

6–12.1—Comprehends a sequence of information on familiar topics as presented through stories, face-to-face conversations, and in contextualized settings.

6–12.2—Produces statements and asks questions on familiar and routine subjects.

Clustered Criteria Checklist

Criteria/Performance Indicators	Not Yet 0	Yes 1
Listening Readiness		
• Am I face-to-face with the speaker?		
• Am I sitting up straight?		
• Am I able to see the speaker and visual aids?		
• Am I holding my pencil and do I have paper ready to take notes?		
• Am I calm, attentive, and ready to listen?		
Listening for Comprehension		
• Am I listening to changes in *intonation, stress,* and *inflection?*		
• Am I making eye contact with the speaker?		
• Am I watching the speaker's motions and gestures?		
• Am I seeing the visual aids?		
• Am I able to connect what the speaker is saying to something I know?		
Showing My Understanding		
• Am I able to retell two main ideas from the presentation?		
• Am I able to ask two appropriate questions to clarify my understanding?		
• Am I able to summarize the presentation and state the main idea?		
• Am I able to use what I have learned?		
Total Points		

Comments:

Scale:

Fulton County ELL Performance Benchmarks. Checklist prepared by ESOL teachers in Fulton County, Georgia. Used with permission.

EXAMPLE

Science Checklist
Earth Science

Clustered Criteria Checklist

Criteria/Performance Indicators	Not Yet 0	Some Evidence 1
The Student . . . **Recognizes and names common earth materials:**		
• soil		
• rocks		
• water		
• air		
Sorts rocks and soils by:		
• color		
• size		
• texture		
Identifies common surface features:		
• oceans		
• lakes		
• mountains		
• rivers		
• forest		
Knows the primary groups of rocks:		
• igneous		
• metamorphic		
• sedimentary		
Compares and contrasts similarities and differences in:		
• rocks		
• minerals		

Student Comments:

Teacher Comments:

Scale:
15–17 = A
13–14 = B
10–12 = C
0–9 = Not Yet

Comparing Mammals and Fish
(Grade 2)

Name: _____ Date: _____

Grade: _____ Teacher: _____

Standard: Completes graphic organizers independently for prewriting planning.

Assignment: Create a Venn diagram comparing mammals and fish.

Clustered Criteria Checklist

Criteria/Performance Indicators	Not Yet 0	Yes 1
Shape of Venn Diagram		
• Do I have 2 large circles?		
• Do they *overlap?*		
• Do I have room to write at least 6 lines in each circle?		
Listing of Characteristics		
• Have I listed *body parts* for each type of animal?		
• Have I listed how they *reproduce?*		
• Have I listed where they *live?*		
• Do I tell how they *move?*		
• Do I tell about *body covering?*		
Content		
• Do I compare *body parts?*		
• Do I understand all the *vocabulary words?*		
• Do I compare *reproduction?*		
• Do I compare *habitats?*		
• Do I compare *ways of moving?*		
• Do I compare *body coverings?*		
Organization and Mechanics		
• Does each of the 3 sections have a title?		
• Are the same *characteristics* listed on *parallel lines?*		
• Are all words spelled correctly?		
Total Points		

Comments:

Scale:	15–17	Satisfactory +
	10–14	Satisfactory
	0–9	Not Yet

Fulton County ELL Performance Benchmarks. Checklist prepared by ESOL teachers in Fulton County, Georgia. Used with permission.

Observation Checklists

Observation Checklists

1. Why do you think checklists are used most often for formative assessments?

_____

_____

_____

_____

_____

_____

_____

_____

_____

Portfolio Checklist
_____ Creative cover
_____ Table of contents
_____ Reflections
_____ Evidence of understanding
_____ Goal setting

2. Comment on why a checklist such as the portfolio checklist shown here is often not enough for a summative evaluation.

_____

_____

_____

_____

_____

_____

_____

_____

GRAPHIC ORGANIZERS

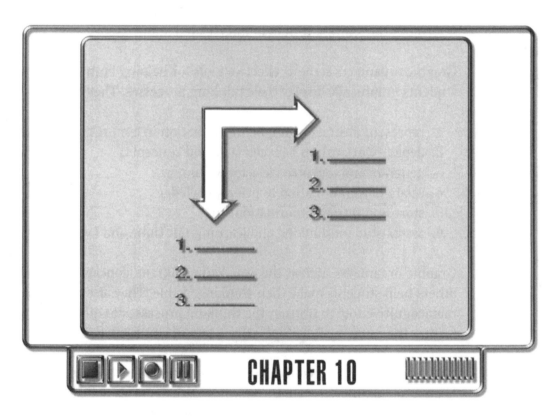

CHAPTER 10

"Graphic organizers embedded in a cooperative environment are more powerful teaching tools than teacher talk or conventional skill drill techniques. The graphic organizers are also tools for more sophisticated and authentic assessment approaches."

—BELLANCA, 1992, P. vi

Graphic Organizers

What Are Graphic Organizers?

Graphic organizers are mental maps that represent key skills like sequencing, comparing and contrasting, and classifying and involve students in active thinking. These mental maps depict complex relationships and promote clearer understanding of content lessons. They also "provide tools to help students organize and find patterns among the overwhelming amount of information available today, as well as to make sense out of it and evaluate it" (Costa, in Hyerle, 1996, p. x).

Graphic organizers help students make their thinking visible.

As Hyerle (1996, p. 11) says "visual tools are for constructing representations of knowledge. In educational terms, visual tools are for constructing and remembering, communicating, and negotiating meanings, and assessing and reforming the shifting terrain of interrelated knowledge."

Graphic organizers serve as effective tools for helping both teachers and students graphically display their thinking processes. They also help

1. represent abstract or implicit information in a more concrete form,
2. depict relationships between facts and concepts,
3. generate and organize ideas for writing,
4. relate new information to prior knowledge,
5. store and retrieve information, and
6. assess student thinking and learning (McTighe and Lyman, 1992, p. 81).

Graphic organizers such as the web, Venn diagram, concept map, and many others help students make their thinking visible. They also "become a metacognitive tool to transfer the thinking processes to other lessons which feature the same relationships" (Black and Black, 1990, p. 2).

In the book *What Works in Schools: Translating Research into Action*, Marzano (2003b) examined the research on categories of instructional strategies that have the greatest effect on student achievement. His metanalysis of the research showed that nonlinquistic representations that ask students to make mental images, pictures, and graphic organizers help students recall what they already know about the content and help them organize or think about the content by synthesizing new information.

Introducing Graphic Organizers

Teachers can do the following when introducing new graphic organizers:

1. Show and explain the new organizer and model how to use it with the whole class by selecting a topic that is easily understood by all of the students (e.g., web of attributes of school lunches).
2. Allow students to practice using the graphic organizer in small groups. Let them select a topic of their choice.
3. Ask individual students to complete a graphic organizer on their own in class or for homework.
4. Encourage students or groups to create an original organizer to share subject content with the class.

Once students become comfortable using a variety of graphic organizers, they will begin to incorporate them in their note taking, projects, and performances.

Students who are visual learners need graphic organizers to help them organize information and remember key concepts.

Why Should We Use Graphic Organizers?

Many students cannot connect or relate new information to prior knowledge because they have trouble remembering things. Graphic organizers help them remember because they function as blueprints or maps that make abstract ideas more visible and concrete. Students also need to make connections between prior knowledge, what they are doing today, and what they can apply or transfer to other things. Graphic organizers help bridge those connections and make them stronger. Students who are visual learners need graphic organizers to help them organize information and remember key concepts.

Vacca (2002) discusses the use of graphic organizers to help students make sense of expository texts. The organizers reflect overarching text patterns such as problem-solution, comparison-contrast, cause-effect description, and sequence. He says that "graphic organizers enable students to identify what ideas in an expository text are important, how these ideas are related, and where to find specific information about these ideas in the text" (p. 10).

Hyerle (1996) states that visual tools like graphic organizers are becoming key teaching, learning, and assessing tools because students are faced with an overwhelming and ever-changing quantity of data they are attempting to synthesize into a quality representation. They are also trying to construct knowledge for themselves and engage in simulation and interactive learning experiences.

Graphic Organizers

How Should We Assess Graphic Organizers?

Graphic organizers have frequently been used in the learning process. Teachers use them to introduce topics, while students use them to study, and sometimes to present important information to other group members. Graphic organizers can also be used as assessment tools to see what students have learned.

Why not ask students to select a graphic organizer to take the place of an essay? Why couldn't students complete a right-angle thinking model listing the facts on the right and their feelings or associations about the topic on the bottom? Why couldn't an English teacher ask her students to fill in a Venn diagram comparing the works of Hemingway and Faulkner? (See example below.) Students could get points for every correct characteristic they feel the authors have in common (middle area) and points for each of the characteristics they feel is different (outside circles). Including graphic organizers on tests would be more creative, challenging, and fun than traditional objective-style items. Teachers could also require students to write a paragraph or make an oral presentation discussing the different elements of the graphic organizer as part of a test.

Graphic organizers can be used as assessment tools.

ASSESSMENT: COMPARISON OF HEMINGWAY AND FAULKNER

Directions:
1. Each correct comparison or difference is worth one point.
2. Write a paragraph comparing and contrasting the two authors. (10 points)

Hemingway

DIFFERENT
1. Grew up in the Midwest
2. Served in World War I
3. Used short sentences and simple style
4. Set major works in Europe, Africa, and Cuba

ALIKE
1. Both won Nobel prizes for literature
2. Both wrote about psychology
3. Both were twentieth-century authors

Faulkner

DIFFERENT
1. Grew up in the South
2. Worked as a scriptwriter in Hollywood
3. Used long sentences and intricate style
4. Set all stories in fictional county in Mississippi

Graphic organizers can be used as assessment tools in the following ways:

1. Include graphic organizers on quizzes and tests.
2. Require groups to complete an assigned graphic organizer and topic on newsprint. Give a group grade for the final graphic organizer and oral presentation.
3. Assign students to select one graphic organizer to use to analyze a lecture, video, book, piece of fiction, piece of nonfiction, speech, news story, or textbook reading. Grade the assignment on accuracy, originality, and creativity.
4. Allow the students to select one or two graphic organizer assignments from their work to include in their portfolios.
5. Assign students to complete a graphic organizer in cooperative groups. Ask each student in each group to complete an individual writing or speaking assignment based on the ideas included in the graphic organizer. Give a group grade and an individual grade.
6. Ask the students or the cooperative group to invent an original graphic organizer. Grade the assignment on the basis of originality, creativity, usefulness, and logic.
7. Require students to utilize a graphic organizer in a project or oral presentation. Grade on the quality and effectiveness of the graphic organizer to enhance the presentation.
8. Create a picture graphic organizer (such as the modified Venn diagram shown below) that includes outlines of objects rather than circles or lines.

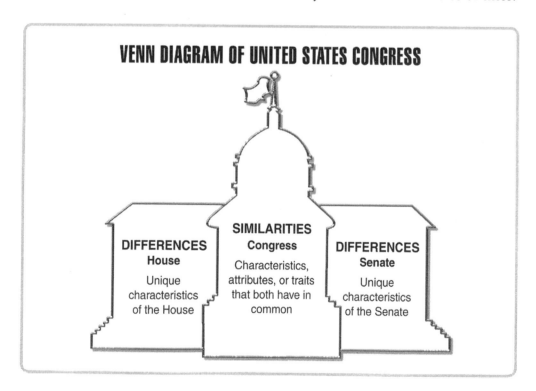

VENN DIAGRAM OF UNITED STATES CONGRESS

SIMILARITIES
Congress

DIFFERENCES
House

Unique characteristics of the House

Characteristics, attributes, or traits that both have in common

DIFFERENCES
Senate

Unique characteristics of the Senate

Graphic Organizers

Tools for the Future

In the world of MTV and rapid-fire television montages, it is no wonder so many students learn best when their visual/spatial intelligence is activated. Students with reading problems or language barriers have difficulty with tests that require only verbal/linguistic and logical/mathematical skills. If today's students are going to construct knowledge for themselves, they will need what Hyerle (1996) describes as dynamic new mental tools. "These tools will help them unlearn and relearn what we have taught them so that they may build new theories of knowledge and also have the experience and capacity to create new tools for making sense of their world" (p. 127).

The following pages provide examples of just a few types of graphic organizers that serve as assessment tools for authentic learning.

EXAMPLES

PRIMARY

VENN DIAGRAM

Tyrannosaurus rex   Polar Bear

Different / Alike \ Different

Different
– Extinct species
– Scales
– Awake all year
– Lived in temperate regions

Alike
– Claws
– Teeth
– Tails
– Eat meat

Different
– Surviving species
– Fur
– Sleeps through winter
– Lives in the Arctic

MIDDLE SCHOOL

MIND MAP

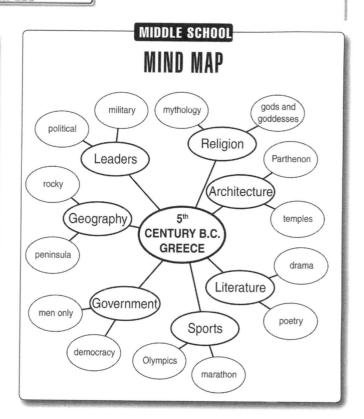

military   mythology   gods and goddesses
political
Leaders   Religion
rocky   Parthenon
                  Architecture
Geography   5th CENTURY B.C. GREECE   temples
peninsula
men only   Government   Literature   drama
democracy   Sports   poetry
         Olympics
         marathon

HIGH SCHOOL

AGREE/DISAGREE CHART

SUBJECT: Health/Physical Education
TOPIC: Alcohol/Drug Unit

STATEMENT	BEFORE		AFTER	
	Agree	Disagree	Agree	Disagree
1. Marijuana is a safe drug.	KB	BR MC		KR BR MC
2. Alcoholism is a disease.	MC	BR KB	MC	BR KB
3. Steroids are legal.	KB BR MC			KB BR MC
4. Crack is not as lethal as cocaine.	KB	BR MC		KB BR MC
5. Alcoholism runs in families.		KB BR MC	KB BR MC	
6. Men can drink more than women.	KB MC	BR	KB BR MC	

COLLEGE

THINKING AT RIGHT ANGLES

SUBJECT: United States History
DIRECTIONS: Complete the thinking at right angles graphic organizer by listing the facts about the topic in section A and your feelings or associations about the topic in section B.

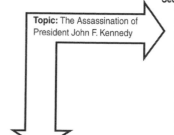

Topic: The Assassination of President John F. Kennedy

Section A (FACTS)
1. November 22, 1963
2. Dallas, Texas
3. Texas governor also shot
4. Kennedy died at Parkland Hospital
5. Johnson sworn in as President
6. Oswald arrested
7. Ruby killed Oswald
8. Funeral in Washington, D.C.
9. Riderless horse
10. Salute by JFK, Jr.

Section B (FEELINGS OR ASSOCIATIONS)
1. Betrayal–Who can we trust?
2. Loss of innocence: Nation experienced tragedy
3. Glued to TV for days: Nation was paralyzed
4. End of Camelot: Death of King Arthur
5. Sadness: Fear of a conspiracy
6. Just the beginning in a series of national tragedies

Graphic Organizers

Agree/Disagree Statements

Directions: Write statements about a topic your students will study. Give this list to groups of students *before* and *after* the unit and ask them to write their initials in the Agree or Disagree columns.

Topic: _____

STATEMENTS	BEFORE		AFTER	
	Agree	Disagree	Agree	Disagree
1.				
2.				
3.				
4.				
5.				
6.				
7.				
8.				
9.				
10.				

Thinking At Right Angles

Directions: Select a topic and ask students to list the facts about it in column A and their feelings and associations in column B.

Topic: _____

FACTS → **A**   FACTS
_____
_____
_____
_____
_____
_____
_____
_____
_____
_____

FEELINGS AND ASSOCIATIONS ↓

B

FEELINGS AND ASSOCIATIONS

_____
_____
_____
_____
_____

Graphic Organizers

1. Take this survey and in the *Before* column check off what you believed about authentic assessment *before* you started to read this book. In the *After* column, check off your answer *after* reading this book.

Agree/Disagree Chart on Authentic Assessment

STATEMENT	BEFORE		AFTER	
	Agree	Disagree	Agree	Disagree
1. Formative assessments are ongoing.				
2. Portfolios always contain final products.				
3. Metacognition is illegal in 23 states.				
4. Letter writing is more authentic than grammar exercises.				
5. Rubrics are puzzle cubes.				

2. Comment on any statement where you changed your opinion and discuss what you have learned that caused you to change your opinion.

INTERVIEWS AND CONFERENCES

CHAPTER 11

"Those who teach understand that, while personal communication is a mode of assessment that virtually never informs the momentous decisions and will never command the attention to our highly visible standardized testing programs, it nevertheless always has been and will be a critical form of classroom assessment."

—STIGGINS, 1994, P. 206

Interviews and Conferences

What Are Interviews and Conferences?

Teachers gather a great deal of valuable information about student achievement by talking with students. During the teaching and learning process, teachers ask questions, listen to answers, conduct conferences and interviews, evaluate student reasoning, conduct oral examinations, and engage in conversations with students (Stiggins, 1994). Some teachers, however, are reluctant to utilize direct personal communication with students as legitimate assessment because they feel it is too subjective. Imagine how shaky a teacher would feel telling a parent, "I have an intuition or gut feeling that Bradley doesn't cooperate effectively." Yet, conferences and interviews structured effectively yield legitimate achievement data as well as monitor students' attitudes and feelings.

Conferences and interviews can be structured to yield legitimate achievement data.

Types of Interviews and Conferences

Teachers utilize a wide variety of both formal and informal interviews and conferences, such as the following:

1. book interview with one student or group of students
2. discussion about a group or an individual project
3. interview about a research paper or project
4. reactions to a film or video
5. feedback on a field trip
6. reactions to assemblies or guest speakers
7. discussion of a piece of writing
8. interview in a foreign language class to check for fluency and grammar in that language
9. feelings about works of art or music composition
10. discussion about problem solving
11. interview about a scientific experiment
12. attitudes about a course or school
13. conference about a portfolio
14. discussion about dynamics of cooperative groups
15. discussion of students' grades and future goals
16. feelings about sportsmanship and ethics
17. interview about procedures
18. questions about the process in a paper or project
19. conversations about meeting standards
20. discussion of grades

Student interviews and conferences reinforce communication. Students should be encouraged to engage in oral interactions on a daily basis, and these authentic assessments provide the opportunity to assess their knowledge, insights, and feelings as qualitative data.

Why Should We Use Interviews and Conferences?

Primary teachers base more assessment on direct personal communication with the student than teachers in the middle school or high school. Sometimes talking to younger students is the most effective way to assess what they know and feel.

The Ministry of Education in British Columbia published a booklet entitled *Supporting Learning: Understanding and Assessing the Progress of Children in the Primary Program.* In a section called "How We Find Out What a Child Can Do," the text reads: "Teachers collect information about a child's progress in the same way that parents collect information about their child's growth and learning. They watch children in action, look at collections of children's work and talk with children. In the Primary Program this is called 'collecting authentic evidence'" (1991b, p. 13).

Sometimes talking to younger students is the most effective way to assess what they know and feel.

If teachers talk with and listen to students, they are able to gather information that sometimes cannot be gathered any other way, no matter what the ages of the learners. When talking with and listening to students, teachers use the experience to:

- help clarify thinking,
- assist children in thinking about their own learning,
- help achieve new levels of understanding,
- facilitate self-evaluation,
- make them feel their ideas and opinions are valued,
- help children appreciate progress and set future goals,
- respond to their comments,
- build positive teacher-child relationships, and
- lead them [students] to become self-directed learners, (Ministry of Education, 1991b, p. 16).

Interviews and Conferences

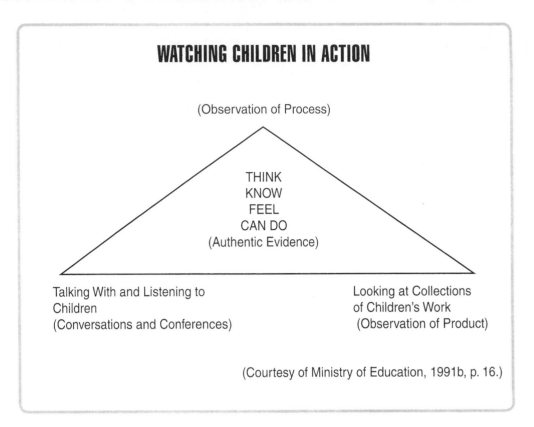

WATCHING CHILDREN IN ACTION

(Observation of Process)

THINK
KNOW
FEEL
CAN DO
(Authentic Evidence)

Talking With and Listening to
Children
(Conversations and Conferences)

Looking at Collections
of Children's Work
(Observation of Product)

(Courtesy of Ministry of Education, 1991b, p. 16.)

The interactions
that take place in
a learner-focused
classroom enhance the
communication skills
of the students.

In interviews, conferences, and conversations, students get the opportunity to refine and clarify their thinking and respond to others. Additionally, talking about what they have done and what they plan to do is essential if students are going to learn how to evaluate themselves. The interactions that take place in a learner-focused classroom enhance the communication skills of the students and provide valuable assessment tools for the teacher.

How Should We Assess Interviews and Conferences?

Some schools are now mandating that teachers conduct conferences with individual students at least once a month. In order to do that, however, elementary teachers would have to conduct one conference a day, and secondary teachers might have to conduct as many as five a day. And what are the other students supposed to be doing when the teacher is conferencing with a student? Many teachers are experimenting with allowing other students to do group work or independent work while they are talking with one student. Some are also conducting group conferences or allowing students to do peer conferences using guiding questions to help the student focus on key points.

Kallick (1992) says that the "quality of the conference is far more significant than the quantity of conferences" (p. 314). She asks teachers to imagine that they are able to resurrect someone like John Dewey or Jean Piaget for only fifteen minutes. Most of the questions would elicit responses that only Dewey or Piaget could provide. Questions like "What was on your mind when . . .?" or "Now that you have accomplished your work, what do you think about . . .?" would yield provocative answers. These types of questions could only be answered by a primary source. Why waste precious time by asking low-level questions like "Where were you born?" or "How did you die?"

The few minutes teachers have with each student should be handled the same way. Higher-order questions that assess the student's thoughts or feelings are more valuable than short-answer recall questions that could be answered on a test or survey.

Sample Questions for Student Interview

- How did you feel about our unit on poetry?
- How do you feel about your writing?
- In your opinion, why is it important to keep a portfolio?
- Do you think you are meeting the standards? Why or why not?
- What are you learning? How can you use your new learning?

Interviews and conferences should play an important role in the assessment process in all classrooms.

Interviews and conferences, therefore, should play an important role in the assessment process in all classrooms—from kindergarten to graduate school. After all, communication skills dominate most state standards, and speaking and listening skills are equally as important as reading and writing skills—not only in school but throughout life.

Interviews and Conferences

EXAMPLES

PRIMARY

TEACHER-STUDENT CONFERENCE

Student: _Bruce_ **Date:** _March 15_

Purpose of Conference:
To discuss Bruce's work with his group

What items were discussed?

1. _frequent absences_
2. _personality conflict with David_
3. _refusal to accept role assignments_

Student's Reaction to Conference: (Complete and return within 2 days)

I stay home from school because I hate my group. David always makes fun of me when I'm the recorder because I can't write well.

Teacher's Reaction to Conference:

I will work with your group on the social skill of helping one another and encouragement. I will also monitor your group more often.

Date and Time to Follow-up Conference: _March 25, 3:30_

MIDDLE SCHOOL

BOOK REVIEW CONFERENCE

Title of book: _To Kill a Mockingbird_

Date: _March 15_ **Grade:** _9_

Ratings:
2 = Strong Evidence
1 = Some Evidence
0 = Not Yet

Scale:
9–10 = A
7–8 = B
5–6 = C
3–4 = Not Yet

The student demonstrates understanding of:	Plot	Setting	Characters	Theme	Symbols	Total Points	Final Grade
1. Ricardo	2	2	2	1	2	9	A
2. Sherry	1	2	1	0	0	4	Not yet
3. Joann	2	2	2	2	2	10	A
4. Rick	1	2	1	1	2	7	B
5. John	2	2	2	1	2	9	A
6. Bruce	1	1	1	0	1	4	Not yet
7. Jose	2	2	2	1	1	8	B
8. Anna	1	1	2	1	2	7	B
9. Vladic	2	2	2	2	2	10	A
10. Frank	2	2	2	1	2	9	A

HIGH SCHOOL

PEER CONFERENCE ON WRITTEN WORK

☑ First Reading ☐ Second Reading ☐ Third Reading

Please read or listen to my written work and help me by answering the following questions:

Title of Piece: _"My Pet Peeves"_

The part I like best is _examples_ because...	_you give specifics like gum chewing—people saying "you know"_
The part I am not really clear about is _why_ because...	_you don't say why you have the pet peeves_
Please tell me more about...	_when you first realized you had these pet peeves_
You might want to try...	_including fewer pet peeves but describing them in more detail_

Written by: _Pablo_ **Read by:** _Jim_

COLLEGE

PROBLEM-SOLVING INTERVIEW

Student: _Lynn_ **Date:** _January 5_

Type of Problem: _We want everyone on the team to compete but we also want to win the debate._

☐ Self Assessment ☑ Peer Assessment ☐ Teacher Assessment

	Yes	Not Yet	Questions
1.	✓		Can you explain the problem?
2.	✓		Can you brainstorm possible solutions?
3.		✓	Can you list steps to solve the problem?
4.	✓		Can you relate this problem to others like it?
5.		✓	Can you give alternative solutions?

Problem:	_We have 8 people on the debate team, but only 4 people can compete._
Best Solution:	_Rotate 4-person teams._
First Step:	_Establish schedule._

ON YOUR OWN

Plan a Portfolio Conference

Directions: Have students create a list of questions they would want their teacher or their parents to ask them during a portfolio conference. Encourage the students to write higher-order questions that elicit reflective responses.

Questions For My Portfolio Conference

1. _____
   _____
   _____

2. _____
   _____
   _____

3. _____
   _____
   _____

4. _____
   _____
   _____

5. _____
   _____
   _____

6. _____
   _____
   _____

Interviews and Conferences

Problem-Solving Interview

Student: _____ **Date:** _____

Problem: _____

_____

☐ Self Assessment ☐ Peer Assessment ☐ Teacher Assessment

	Yes 0	Not Yet 1	Questions
1.			Can you explain the problem?
2.			Can you speculate what you think the real problem is?
3.			Can you brainstorm two possible solutions?
4.			Can you evaluate your solutions and select the best one?
5.			Can you describe two steps you will take to solve the problem?

Two Possible Solutions
1. 2.

Best Solution

Two Steps to Solve Problem
1. 2.

ON YOUR OWN

Peer Conference on Written Work

Directions: Have student exchange their written work with a partner and critique the work by using the following form.

☐ First Reading ☐ Second Reading ☐ Third Reading

Please read or listen to my written work and help me by answering the following questions:

Title of Piece: _____

The part I like best is _____ because...

The part I am not really clear about is _____ because...

Please tell me more about...

You might want to try...

Written by: _____ **Read by:** _____

Date: _____ **Date:** _____

Interviews and Conferences

Interview on Student Projects

Student: _____ **Date:** _____

Subject Area: _____

1. Describe your project.

   _____
   _____
   _____

2. Why did you select this project?

   _____
   _____
   _____

3. What do you like best about your project?

   _____
   _____
   _____

4. If you could do anything differently, what would it be?

   _____
   _____
   _____

5. What skills or knowledge from other subject areas did you use to complete this project?

   _____
   _____
   _____

6. What have you learned about yourself by completing this project?

   _____
   _____
   _____

7. What skills, concepts, or insights have you learned from completing this project?

   _____
   _____
   _____

Teacher's Signature: _____

Interviews and Conferences

1. Reflect on the value of utilizing personal communication to find out what students know and how they feel. Do you agree or disagree with Stiggins (1994, p. 206) that "personal communication always has been and will be a critical form of classroom assessment?" Explain.

_____

_____

_____

_____

_____

_____

_____

_____

2. Brainstorm four ways you can use personal communication as a valuable assessment tool.

- _____

_____

- _____

_____

- _____

_____

- _____

_____

THE FINAL GRADE

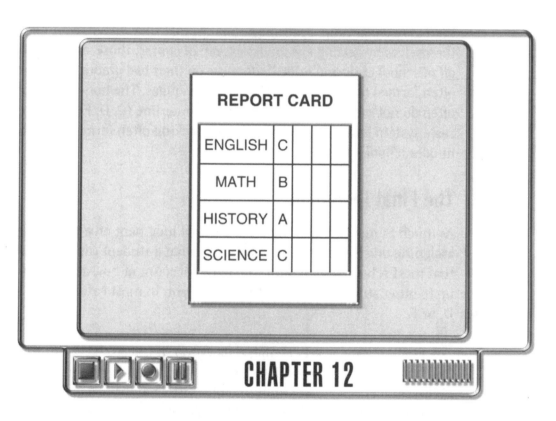

REPORT CARD

ENGLISH	C			
MATH	B			
HISTORY	A			
SCIENCE	C			

CHAPTER 12

"Schools and teachers have a responsibility to communicate effectively with parents and others who are interested in the progress of students. Traditionally, report cards with letter or percentage grades and brief comments have been the main vehicles for communication. This has led to a cult-like status for grades, but grades are only part of the communication system."

—O'CONNOR, 1999, P. 168

The Final Grade

What Are Final Grades?

"No level of education is free from it; no teacher or student can hide from it. The cry of 'Wad-Ja-Get?' is all around us . . . Students, from kindergarten through graduate school, feel the ache of the 'Wad-Ja-Get?' syndrome; most know that it dominates more of their learning than they would ever care to admit" (Simon & Bellanca, 1976, p. 1). Although this statement appeared in 1976, it still characterizes the type of competitive, bottom-line, win-at-any-cost mentality that is prevalent in schools and society. Students learn at an early age that they should get good grades if they want to impress and please their teachers and their parents

Students learn at an early age that they should get good grades if they want to impress and please their teachers and their parents.

Getting all As on the report card is more important to most students than their love of learning. Students also know that they do not want to embarrass themselves by getting low grades except, of course, those students who turn off of school early and pride themselves on their bad grades. Peer groups are often formed on the basis of grade point averages. The honor roll students often do not mix well with the remedial borderline (C, D, F) students. A type of caste system based on report cards and tracking often forms in schools by the middle school years.

The Final Judgment

As much as most teachers hate to pass final judgment on a student by assigning one letter grade to summarize what a student can do, the reality is that most school systems still demand an account of how a student measures up to other students—and that measurement, in most cases, is still an A, B, C, D, or F.

The grading issue is very complex; moreover, it is also steeped in tradition. Teachers have been forced to become bean counters by adding up all the grades, bonus points, and minus points before using the calculator to divide by the total number of entries—to the second decimal point, of course. It's always amazing to see how much a student's final grade is lowered when the teacher adds in all those minus points and zeros for missing homework assignments, forgetting to bring books, writing with pencil instead of pen and—the ultimate—for using spiral notebook paper instead of loose-leaf paper! Sound ludicrous? Ask teachers and students if they have ever experienced or heard about these types of situations. Many people have lost points or received an F for writing on the back of the paper or forgetting to put their name on assignments. To say that the grading system in many American schools is archaic, inconsistent, and whimsical may be an understatement. The final or summative grades in any course are probably the most difficult to assign because despite a student's rate of learning, ability level, special needs, or learning styles, he or she still has to be judged.

Emphasis on Grades

The final grade in a course or year carries tremendous weight. The grade could determine promotion or retention, participation in extracurricular activities, induction into an honor society, earning a college scholarship, or graduating from high school. Yet, it is difficult to sum up all the multiple levels of learning and all the objectives or standards covered in a course with one letter or number grade.

A few educators advocate giving several final grades. For example, a report card might contain three grades—one grade to represent how a student has improved individually, the second to show how he or she compares to other students in the same grade level, and the third to represent how the student is doing compared to standards set by the district, state, or nation based on benchmarks or exemplary performances.

Some districts' new report cards narrate how students have achieved learning standards as well as set new goals.

Some districts have eliminated traditional letter grades at the primary level, and some others have eliminated them through eighth grade. The new report cards narrate how students have achieved learning standards as well as set new goals. Across the country, the traditional report card is gradually changing to reflect portfolio assessments, student-led conferences, anecdotal reports, narrative summaries, continuum of progress reports, student self-assessments, observation checklists, and other performance-based and more qualitative ways to assess student growth and development.

Why Do We Need to Change Our Grading System?

According to Cizek,"The task of reforming educational assessment has just begun. New forms of assessment cannot provide clearer or more complete information about student achievement unless the ways in which achievement is communicated are replaced. The real challenge for assessment reform will be to bring assessment and grading practices into the fold" (1996, as cited in O'Connor, 1999, p. 147).

The Final Grade

Importance of Self-Concept

The personal discovery of meaning by a student includes his or her feelings, attitudes, values, beliefs, hopes, and desires. This subjective experience, however, has to be objectified—broken down into discrete objectives and skills and correlated to standards—before it is meshed into one final grade. In this process, the self-concept of the student often suffers.

"We now understand that an individual's self-concept determines his or her behavior in almost everything that person does. It also affects intelligence, for people who believe they are *able* will try, while those who believe they are *unable* will not" (Combs, 1976, p. 7).

Combs also explains that people derive their self-concept from the feedback they receive from the people who surround them while they are growing up. Teachers provide much of that feedback via written and oral communication and, of course, grades. Poor grades, especially as early as kindergarten and first grade, have a negative impact on a student. Moreover, classification in a lower track exacerbates the student's poor self-concept because now not only do the teacher and student recognize the problem but everybody—counselors, parents, students, other teachers, and administrators—knows the student has a "problem." How many students have been negatively influenced by feedback from teachers? And, most important, how many times has this negative feedback in the form of comments and grades become a self-fulfilling prophecy for the student?

Competition

In addition to the inequities in the grading system and the damage grades cause to the self-concept of many students, the emphasis on competition to achieve higher grades or higher groups also weakens the learning process. Competition for grades, reading groups, honor rolls, and scholarships probably *weakens* the educational system because it separates the winners from the losers. First graders learn early on that the "robin" reading groups are the winners and the "buzzards" are the losers.

Kohn (1992) attacks the sacred cow of competition by stating that competition is not part of human nature. Instead, competition poisons relationships, hurts self-esteem, and impedes excellence. If students constantly compete for the highest grade in the class, the honor roll, or for class valedictorian, they often lose sight of one of the most thoughtful outcomes of all—collaboration.

How many times has negative feedback become a self-fulfilling prophecy for the student?

How can students be taught to cooperate with group members, share, teach each other, and compromise when their major concern is to beat out everyone else, get ahead, come out on top, and, at all costs, win?

Contrary to a long-held American belief, individuals who work alone, compete against everyone around them, and value winning above all else do not necessarily come out on top, nor do they necessarily make good students or employees. Report after report from business leaders and from the SCANS report issued by the United States Department of Labor (1992) stress the importance of cooperation in the workplace. People who listen to others, work together, share ideas, and cooperate often contribute more to the overall effectiveness of a company than most individualistic, competitive people. Therefore, educators and parents who emphasize competition, high grades at any cost, and the ultimate weapon—the grading curve—may be doing a disservice to students. A major paradigm shift needs to occur so that society values cooperation—not competition.

Goleman (1995) talks about the importance of emotional intelligence and how the emotional lessons students learn at school help shape the temperament and emotional habits that will govern their lives. He advocates an educational system that routinely inculcates "essential human competencies such as self-awareness, self-control, and empathy, and the arts of listening, resolving conflicts, and cooperation" (p. xiv). These traits are a more accurate prediction of a person's success in life, and they should be nurtured by educators.

Competition for grades probably *weakens* the educational system because it separates the winners from the losers.

Cheating

Another reason the current grading system must be reevaluated and reformed is the fact that it leads to cheating—an inevitable by-product of the grading system. Cheating in American schools is epidemic. Many students from kindergarten through college engage in cheating to pass a course or get a higher grade. Cheating involves plagiarizing term papers or book reports, copying another's test answers, talking to other students who took the test, stealing tests or a teacher's edition of a book, or altering grades in a grade book. These acts may be attributed, at least in part, to too much pressure being placed on students to make the grade.

The Final Grade

Students will often cheat to:

1. avoid failing a test
2. avoid being branded stupid by peers
3. avoid punishment by parents (losing privileges)
4. be able to try out for the team or cheerleading squad
5. participate in extracurricular activities
6. get on the honor roll
7. avoid being sent to remedial classes
8. get accepted to college
9. win a scholarship to college
10. get a thrill

The current grading system exerts enormous pressure on many students.

The current grading system exerts enormous pressure on many students to compete and sometimes to cheat in order to succeed. Posting grades on the blackboard; publishing honor rolls; awarding bonus points, candy, free recess, or field trips for high scores; assigning students to gifted classes on the basis of test scores; and honoring students who receive the highest grades at school-wide assemblies promote a heavy emphasis on the grading process.

Education needs to be both a quantifiable objective process as well as a qualitative affective process. At a very early age, students learn to cope with the system, and by the time they get to high school, Glasser (1986) says as many as 50 percent of secondary students have become what he calls "unsatisfied students." The unsatisfied student makes no consistent effort to learn. "All living creatures, and we are no exception, only do what they believe is most satisfying to them, and the main reason our schools are less effective than we would like them to be is that, where students are concerned, we have failed to appreciate this fact" (p. 8).

By the time a student gets to high school, he or she may have faced hundreds of humiliations because of low grades. It is no wonder self-concept suffers and many students choose to act out, drop out, or cheat to escape the endless pressure to pass. In addition, the frustration of trying hard but still receiving poor grades (or not meeting the standards or not scoring well on the standardized tests) because of learning or behavior disabilities discourages and frustrates many students. The pressure to collect, analyze, and compare grades overrides the needs of the students to construct knowledge for themselves, to achieve true understanding of important concepts, and to enjoy learning and the learning process.

Pressure on Educators

Local newspapers publish standardized test scores. Principals' and superintendents' reputations and jobs are sometimes built and lost on test scores. Realtors often quote the rankings of neighborhood schools when they are trying to sell homes. The pressure is felt not only by students but also by teachers and administrators. The temptation to cheat can move beyond the classroom right into competition between schools and districts to get the top scores on state and national tests. Perhaps it is not so shocking that periodically, scandals appear about teachers coaching students for tests or principals prompting teachers to encourage some low-achieving students to stay home on test day.

An unhealthy emphasis on competition, the need to be number one, standardized test scores, meeting standards, and high grades could backfire and actually be detrimental to the learning process. Cash bonuses, special privileges, and honors for teachers whose students perform well on standardized tests or punishments such as withdrawal of funds from teachers and schools who don't show improvement represent dangerous practices some states are now implementing. The time will come when good teachers refuse to take challenging students or classes and good principals refuse to lead challenging schools because they don't want to risk losing their cash bonuses or, perhaps, their jobs!

An unhealthy emphasis on competition could backfire and be detrimental to the learning process.

How Can We Change the Grading System?

Even if educators agree that the present grading system evolved into a hydra-headed monster that has overshadowed, intimidated, and, in some cases, debilitated students, the fact remains that in most cases the elimination of traditional letter and number grades on report cards is not yet a reality. For most teachers, district mandates, college requirements, and parental pressures dictate that grades in some form are a nonnegotiable requirement. Some districts are required to give grades, are there ways to give more authentic grades that measure growth, development, and performance on the learning standards established at the beginning of the year? Are there ways to give grades to help students to grow and learn rather than to compete in the "Wad-Ja-Get?" contest?

The Final Grade

Grading Options

The following grading options can be used alone or in combination with other options to arrive at a final evaluation:

1. **Anecdotal Report Card**

   The Ministry of Education in British Columbia has used a primary progress report that provides a narrative report on the front and a list of the primary program goals and criteria on the back.

Are there ways to give grades to help students to grow rather than to help them to compete in the "Wad-Ja-Get?" contest?

Anecdotal Report Card

MINISTRY OF EDUCATION: PRIMARY PROGRESS REPORT

Student's Name: _____

School: _____ **District:** _____

Reporting Period: _____ **Date:** _____

The goals of the primary program are to provide a variety of experiences that foster the child's:

- aesthetic and artistic development;
- physical development;
- emotional and social development;
- social responsibility; and
- intellectual development.

Review how the student is doing in each of these areas.

Reommendation: The student should:

☐ Continue in the Primary Program

☐ Begin the Intermediate Program

Parents: Please keep this copy and return the report card cover only. Thank you.

(Source: Courtesy of the Ministry of Education, Province of British Columbia.)

---

2. The Traditional Grade

Each assignment is graded according to specific, predetermined criteria. Once all the grades from assignments, projects, performances, and tests are entered into the gradebook, the teacher adds all the scores and divides by the total number of scores to determine the final grade.

The Traditional Grade

COURSE: AMERICAN LITERATURE

Tests, Assignments, Projects	Grade
1. Test on Puritan unit	94
2. Learning logs	90
3. Reflective journals	93
4. Observation checklist on social skills	85
5. Exhibition of Salem witch trial	96
6. Colonial newspaper project	91
7. Group project on Hawthorne	88
8. Test on *The Scarlett Letter*	83
9. Portfolio	90
	810 points

810 points divided by 9 = 90
Final Grade = 90 (B+)

3. Assessment of Learning Standards

A checklist provides information about whether or not or to what degree students have met individual benchmarks within a standard. The report card could include learning standards and benchmarks. Making a commitment to link standards also means making a commitment to report progress in relation to those standards. According to Carr and Harris (2001), many school districts redesign their reporting systems to report on individual student learning related to the standards and the performance of the school or district as a whole. Carr and Harris believe that the "process of linking standards provides schools and districts the opportunity to reconstruct reporting about individual student learning so that parents, educators, and students share meaningful, useful information" (p. 103).

Assessment of Learning Standards

STANDARDS

Ratings:	0	1	2	3	4
	Novice	In Progress	Almost Meets Standards	Meets Standards	Exceeds Standards

School: _____ Semester: _____

English (0–4)   Final Grade ☐
_____ 1. Demonstrates competence in writing process.
_____ 2. Demonstrates competence in style and rhetoric.
_____ 3. Uses grammatical and mechanical conventions.
_____ 4. Gathers and uses information for research.
_____ 5. Demonstrates competence in speaking and listening.

American History (0–4)   Final Grade ☐
_____ 1. Understands why America attracted Europeans.
_____ 2. Understands how political, religious, and social
          institutions emerged in the English colonies.
_____ 3. Understands how slavery reshaped life in America.

Mathematics (0–4)   Final Grade ☐
_____ 1. Uses a variety of strategies in the problem-solving
          process.
_____ 2. Understands and applies basic and advanced properties
          of the concepts of numbers.
_____ 3. Uses basic and advanced procedures while performing
          the processes of computation.

Technology (0–4)   Final Grade ☐
_____ 1. Identifies basic computer hardware.
_____ 2. Uses menu options and commands.
_____ 3. Knows word processing skills.
_____ 4. Knows characteristics of software programs.

4. Graded Portfolios

Even though some educators do not think a student portfolio should be assigned a grade, many educators, especially at the middle school or high school level, find they motivate students more when the final portfolio is graded. They give regular grades throughout the class for quizzes, tests, homework, and other assignments. However, the portfolio at the end of the course is given a final grade that is usually weighted higher (20 to 25 percent of the total grade). Students, therefore, might not do well on traditional quizzes and tests, but they have a chance to work hard and still succeed by showing improvement on the portfolio.

Graded Portfolio

FINAL PORTFOLIO

Student: _Carol B._   **Class:** _Geometry_   **Date:** _May 26_

Selections	Grade	Comments
1. Geometric drawings	95	You have done a beautiful job drawing and labeling the angles.
2. Research report on *Why Math*	92	The research you did on the relevance of math to our lives helped you see its importance.
3. Learning logs	90	I can see how you were having problems understanding the new concepts.
4. Reflective journals	94	Your frustration on tests is evident from your journal. You seem to be working through your anxiety.
5. Problem-solving logs	75	You still need to explore alternative solutions when you can't solve a problem.
6. Profile of math-related professions	91	You made the transfer of math from the classroom to the outside world.
7. Student self-evaluation for course*	89	I gave myself an 89 because I like math, but I still can't solve problems on my own.
Total Points 626 ÷ 7 = 89.4	**Final Grade** 89	It's interesting that your average is the same as your own self-evaluation!

*Self-evaluation grade is provided by the student

Comments: Your writing and research skills and appreciation of why math is important are excellent. Even though you feel math is your weakest subject, you are making great strides to overcome your phobia and solve problems.

Suggested Future Goals: Work with your cooperative group more. Ask them to "talk out loud" when they are solving problems so you can see their thought processes.

Final portfolio grade = _89_ (50%)
Average grade for other work = _83_ (50%)
Final grade for class = _86 (B)_   Teacher: _Lois Meyers_

The Final Grade

One option in grading the final portfolio includes assigning a separate grade to each item included in the portfolio and then averaging the grades to arrive at a final portfolio grade.

Another option involves asking the students to include 10 to 12 items in their final portfolios, but then the teacher and the students create a rubric that correlates to the unit that was studied. The mythology unit suggested in Chapter 3 could have a rubric similar to the example below. The three grades are averaged to arrive at a final grade. This option takes less time, allows for the teacher to select items to meet the standards, and allows for the students to select items that meet their multiple intelligences and gives them choice.

A third option involves creating a rubric for the portfolio that includes criteria to measure the content, organization, and quality of the whole portfolio without grading each assignment separately. These criteria can also be weighted. The example in Chapter 4, page 71, illustrates this option.

PORTFOLIO RUBRIC FOR MYTHOLOGY UNIT

☒ Self   ☐ Peer   ☐ Teacher

	Hades 1	Parthenon 2	Mt. Olympus (3)
1. Creative cover	The Underworld Gazette	The Athens Chronicle	The Olympus Sun
	1	2	(3)
2 Completeness	Minotaur (half man, half bull)	Perseus (half man, half god)	Zeus (all god)
	1	(2)	3
3. Form (spelling, grammar, punctuation, sentence structure)	Dionysus (sloppy—god of wine)	Odysseus (needs help—phone home)	Hermes (great—god of alphabet)
	1	(2)	3
4. Creativity	Touched by mere mortals	Touched by the demigods	Touched by the god of creativity
	1	2	(3)
5. Evidence of understanding	Hercules (Where are my Cliff Notes?)	Apollo (I see the light!)	Athena (goddess of wisdom)
	1	2	(3)
6. Reflection	Medusa (never uses a mirror)	Narcissus (gazes at own image only)	Aphrodite (reflects in mirror on regular basis)

Comments: I know I still need to work on my sentence structure, but sometimes it gets in the way of creativity. I really don't get grammar rules. They're Greek to me!

Total Points 16 = A

Scale: Total 18 pts
15–18 = A
10–14 = B
6 – 9 = C
Not Yet

From *The Portfolio Connection: Student Work Linked to Standards,* 2nd ed., p. 226, by Burke, K., Fogarty, R., & Belgrad, S. © 2002 SkyLight Professional Development. Reprinted with permission of LessonLab, Glenview, IL.

Reporting Systems

Critics of the traditional A-B-C report card know that a letter grade by itself cannot convey the complexity of the tasks, skills, and standards students are asked to demonstrate. Yet efforts to reform traditional report cards must include all the stakeholders—students, teachers, parents, administrators—if they are going to be accepted and successful. The whole purpose of assessment is to provide feedback to the students and parents about how well students are doing in meeting their objectives, goals, or standards. The grading system used needs to reflect this purpose and honor the dignity of the student. Tomlinson (2001) believes that report cards should show individual growth and relative standing to students and parents: "for example, that an A means excellent growth, a B means very good growth, a C means some growth, and an F means no observable growth—coupled with a notation that a 1 means the student is working above grade level in the subject, a 2 means the student is working at grade level in the subject, and a 3 means the student is working below grade level in a subject. A student might then, for example, earn an A1 or a B2 in reading or science, indicating both the student's personal growth and the student's standing relative to peers or curriculum benchmarks" (pp. 14–15). Report cards should use checklists of escalating competencies that allow teachers to report progress, combined with notations of where students of similar age generally perform on those checklists.

Grades play an integral part of a student's educational journey, as long as they allow for measuring a student's individual growth to achieve the curriculum goals, meet the standards, and understand important concepts about learning and life.

A letter grade by itself cannot convey the complexity of the tasks, skills, and standards students are asked to demonstrate.

The Final Grade

PRIMARY

PROGRESS REPORT

Grade: _First_

Student: _Juan Carlos_

Marking Period: _Weeks 1–12_

	First 6 Weeks			Second 6 Weeks		
	Not Yet	With Support	Independently	Not Yet	With Support	Independently
SPEAKING BEHAVIOR						
Communicates		✓				✓
Speaks in logical sequence			✓			✓
Participates		✓			✓	
LISTENING BEHAVIOR						
Listens to speaker		✓			✓	
Responds appropriately			✓			✓
Asks key questions		✓				✓

COMMENTS: Juan has developed good speaking skills, but he still needs to work on listening to his group members.

MIDDLE SCHOOL

PROGRESS REPORT

Student: _Eric Smith_   **Grade:** _8th_

Attendance	1	2	3	4
Days Present	60	55	50	52
Days Absent	0	5	10	8
Days Tardy	0	3	5	3

Quarter

GRADING SCALE
M = Most of the Time
S = Sometimes
N = Not Yet

	QUARTER			
	1	2	3	4
ENGLISH				
• Makes predictions	S	S	S	S
• Demonstrates active interest	M	S	S	S
• Able to speak in front of groups	M	M	M	M
• Listens to and follows directions	S	M	S	M
PHYSICAL EDUCATION				
• Performs skills well	N	S	S	M
• Positive attitude and effort	N	N	S	S
MATHEMATICS				
• Demonstrates concept of numbers	M	M	M	M
• Demonstrates computational skills	N	S	S	S
• Demonstrates measurement skills	S	S	S	S
ART				
• Performs skills well	M	M	M	M
• Positive attitude and effort	M	M	M	M

HIGH SCHOOL

REPORT CARD

Student: _Betina Gregory_   **Grade:** _11_

English   Final Grade **C**

Writing, Listening, and Speaking (0–4)

 _2_ 1. Demonstrates competence in writing process.
 _2_ 2. Demonstrates competence in style and rhetoric.
 _3_ 3. Uses grammatical and mechanical conventions.
 _2_ 4. Gathers and uses information for research.
 _3_ 5. Demonstrates competence in speaking and listening.

American History (0–4)   Final Grade **B**

 _3_ 1. Understands why America attracted Europeans.
 _3_ 2. Understands how political, religious, and social institutions emerged in the English colonies.
 _2_ 3. Understands how slavery reshaped life in America.

Math (0–4)   Final Grade **A**

 _4_ 1. Uses a variety of strategies in the problem-solving process.
 _3_ 2. Understands and applies basic and advanced properties of the concepts of numbers.
 _4_ 3. Uses basic and advanced procedures while performing the processes of computation.

COLLEGE

REPORT CARD

Student: _Michael Brown_   **Semester:** _2nd_

ECONOMICS   Grade: _B_
Strengths: Budget planning, inflation

Areas to develop: Understanding of different economic systems
Teacher: Ruth Jones

BIOLOGY   Grade: _C_
Strengths: Classification, analysis, problem solving

Areas to develop: Writing effective lab reports
Teacher: Chris Roberts

CIVICS   Grade: _A_
Strengths: Government agencies, state and local governments

Areas to develop: The US election process at the national level
Teacher: Bob Adams

ON YOUR OWN

Report Card Revision

Develop a standards-based report card by stating the standard and creating criteria or benchmarks to assess the standard.

Standard: _____

Criteria or Benchmarks:

1. _____

2. _____

3. _____

4. _____

Standard: _____

Criteria or Benchmarks:

1. _____

2. _____

3. _____

4. _____

The Final Grade

Final Grade Plan

Develop a method to assign weight to the following items and to arrive at a final grade.

Evidence	Weight or Point Value	Rationale
Bringing books and supplies to class		
Daily homework assignments		
Teacher-made tests		
Portfolio		
Group project		
Individual performance		
Final exam		
TOTAL	100%	

Comments:

The Final Grade

1. How do you feel about including effort, attitude, and behavior in the final grade? Explain.

_____

_____

_____

_____

_____

_____

_____

_____

_____

2. Reflect on the grading process currently in place in your school. Offer suggestions to improve the process.

_____

_____

_____

_____

_____

_____

_____

_____

_____

CONCLUSION

"Understanding . . . involves sophisticated insights and abilities, reflected in varied performances and contexts . . . We also suggest that different kinds of understandings exist, that knowledge and skill do not automatically lead to understanding, that misunderstanding is a bigger problem than we realize, and that assessment of understanding therefore requires evidence that cannot be gained from traditional testing alone" (Wiggins and McTighe, 1998, p. 5).

This quotation points out a very important problem in education. Despite all the emphasis on standards, standardized tests, revised curriculum, performance tasks, rubrics, portfolios, and exhibitions, how do educators really know if students *understand* the essential concepts? How do educators recognize and assess the depth of that understanding? And, most important, how can educators clear up misunderstandings? Students memorize facts and demonstrate skills, but do they really understand *why* they are doing these actions?

How do educators recognize and assess the depth of students' understanding of essential concepts?

Wiggins and McTighe (1998, p. 44) identify six facets to describe the levels of understanding. When students truly understand, they:

1. Can *explain:* provide thorough, supported, and justifiable accounts of phenomena, facts, and data.
2. Can *interpret:* tell meaningful stories; offer apt translations; provide a revealing historical or personal dimension to ideas and events; make it personal or accessible through images, anecdotes, analogies, and models.
3. Can *apply:* effectively use and adapt what we know in diverse contexts.
4. Have *perspective:* see and hear points of view through critical eyes and ears; see the big picture.
5. Can *empathize:* find value in what others might find odd, alien, or implausible; perceive sensitively on the basis of prior direct experience.
6. Have *self-knowledge:* perceive the personal style, prejudices, projections, and habits of mind that both shape and impede our own understanding; aware of what they do not understand and why understanding is so hard.

From *Understanding by Design* by Grant Wiggins and Jay McTighe. Alexandria, VA: Association for Supervision and Curriculum Development (44). Reprinted with permission. All rights reserved.

Conclusion

The six levels of understanding provide a taxonomy that ranges from the lowest level of recall to the highest level—knowledge of self. The ancient Greek playwrights used a powerful theme of "know thyself" in their dramas. Costa describes intelligent behavior as "knowing what to do when you don't know what to do." If curriculum, instruction, and assessment integrate to allow students to attain these levels of understanding, then teachers will be able to go way beyond "teaching for the test" or "meeting the standards."

If educators begin with the end in mind and aim for thorough understanding of knowledge and self, than it is imperative that they develop curriculum units and assessment tasks to guide instruction to meet these goals.

If the schools of the twenty-first century are to succeed in meeting the needs of their students, they must go beyond standardized testing.

The assessment ideas in this book represent the tip of the iceberg. If the schools of the twenty-first century plan to succeed in meeting the needs of their students, they must go beyond standardized testing; go beyond worksheets and chapter tests; and go beyond meeting the standards. Teachers must teach for understanding. The educated student of tomorrow, like Cathy—the student pictured at the end of the introduction to this book, must be able to go beyond explaining, interpreting, and applying. She must also be able to develop her own perspective of the world, empathize with others, develop a sense of self-knowledge about her strengths and weaknesses, and recognize her prejudices that could impede her understanding. It is self-awareness that helps her become an *independent learner.*

Independent learners do not need a teacher with a red pen following them through life. They rank at the highest level of understanding—the ability to self-evaluate. The ultimate goal of education is for students to be able to analyze their own actions: What did I do well? If I did this again, what would I do differently? Do I need help? Where do I go if I don't know what to do? The abilities to analyze, make decisions, access information, solve problems, and recognize bias or prejudice provide life skills that go way beyond the memorization of capital cities and the periodic table.

Facts change. Content changes. Standards change. Processing and reasoning skills and teaching for understanding, however, lasts a lifetime. Letter grades, report cards, and class ranks will probably become obsolete. Teachers become facilitators who help students achieve deeper understanding and refine their ability to assess, redirect, and reformulate their own work.

Costa and Kallick (1992) summarize in two sentences the entire purpose of assessment and evaluation: "We must constantly remind ourselves that the ultimate purpose of evaluation is to have students become self-evaluating. If students graduate from our schools still dependent upon others to tell them when they are adequate, good, or excellent, then we've missed the whole point of what education is about" (p. 280).

The purpose of the balanced approach to assessment is to help teachers develop strategies that facilitate student learning. The assessment strategies in this book represent scaffolding that helps the learners internalize the criteria for quality work. The ultimate purpose of evaluation is to help students become independent learners. When curriculum, instruction, and assessment support authentic learning, students become empowered to develop into lifelong learners who can attain deep understanding and self-awareness. The classic Greek playwrights' theme of "know thyself" from the fifth century B.C. continues to be a powerful theme for education in the new millennium.

REFERENCES

Airasian, P. W. (1994). *Classroom assessment* (2nd ed.). New York: McGraw-Hill.

Amrein, A. L. & Berliner, D. C. (2003). The effects of high-stakes testing on student motivation and learning. *Educational Leadership, 60*(5), 32–42.

Archbald, D. A. & Newmann, F. M. (1988). *Beyond standardized testing: Assessing authentic academic achievement in the secondary school.* Madison: University of Wisconsin, National Association of Secondary School Principals.

Ardovino, J., Hollingsworth, J. & Ybarra, S. (2000). *Multiple measures: Accurate ways to assess student achievement.* Thousand Oaks, CA: Corwin Press.

Barell, J. (1992). Like an incredibly hard algebra problem: Teaching for metacognition. In A. L. Costa, J. A. Bellanca & R. Fogarty (Eds.), *If minds matter: A foreword to the future, Volume I* (pp. 257–266). Palatine, IL: IRI/Skylight Publishing.

Barell, J. (1995). *Teaching for thoughtfulness: Classroom strategies to enhance intellectual development* (2nd ed.). White Plains, NY: Longman.

Baron, M. A. & Boschee, F. (1995). *Authentic assessment: The key to unlocking student success.* Lancaster, PA: TECHNOMIC.

Bednar, A. K., Cunningham, D., Duffy, T. M. & Perry, J. D. (1993). Theory into practice: How do we link? In G. Anglin (Ed.), *Instructional technology: Past, present, and future.* Denver, CO: Libraries Unlimited.

Belanoff, P. & Dickson, M. (Eds.). (1991). *Portfolios: Process and product.* Portsmouth, NH: Boynton/Cook Publishers.

Bellanca, J. A. (1992a). Classroom 2001: Evolution, not revolution. In A. L. Costa, J. A. Bellanca & R. Fogarty (Eds.), *If minds matter: A foreword to the future, Volume II* (pp. 161–165). Palatine, IL: IRI/Skylight Publishing.

Bellanca, J. A. (1992b). *The cooperative think tank II: Graphic organizers to teach thinking in the cooperative classroom.* Palatine, IL: IRI/Skylight Publishing.

Bellanca, J. A. (1992c). How to grade (if you must). In A. L. Costa, J. A. Bellanca & R. Fogarty (Eds.), *If minds matter: A foreword to the future, Volume II* (pp. 297–311). Palatine, IL: IRI/ Skylight Publishing.

Bellanca, J. A. & Fogarty, R. (1986). *Catch them thinking: A handbook of classroom strategies.* Palatine, IL: IRI/Skylight Publishing.

Bellanca, J. A. & Fogarty, R. (2003). *Blueprints for achievement in the cooperative classroom* (3rd ed.). Glenview, IL: SkyLight Professional Development.

Bender, W. N. (2002). *Differentiating instruction for students with learning disabilities: Best teaching practices for general and special educators.* Thousand Oaks, CA: Corwin Press.

Benjamin, A. (2002). *Differentiated instruction: A guide for middle and high school teachers.* Larchmont, NY: Eye on Education.

Benson, B. P. (2003). *How to meet standards, motivate students, and still enjoy teaching.* Thousand Oaks, CA: Corwin Press.

References

Black, H. & Black, S. (1990). *Organizing thinking: Graphic organizers, Book II.* Pacific Grove, CA: Midwest Publications Critical Thinking Press and Software.

Board of Education for the City of Etobicoke. (1987). *Making the grade: Evaluating student progress.* Scarborough, Ontario, Canada: Prentice-Hall Canada.

Bracey, G. W. (1998). *Put to the test: An educator's and consumer's guide to standardized testing.* Bloomington, IN: Center for Professional Development and Services, Phi Delta Kappa International.

Brandt, R. (1992a). On performance assessment: A conversation with Grant Wiggins. *Educational Leadership, 49*(8), 35–37.

Brandt, R. (1992b). Overview: A fresh focus for curriculum. *Educational Leadership, 49*(8), 7.

Breaking ranks: Changing an American institution. A *Bulletin* special. (1996). *NASSP Bulletin, 80*(578), 55–66.

Brooks, J. G. (2002). *Schooling for life: Reclaiming the essence of learning.* Alexandria, VA: Association for Supervision and Curriculum Development.

Brooks, J. G. & Brooks, M. G. (1993). *In search of understanding: The case for constructivist classrooms.* Alexandria, VA: Association for Supervision and Curriculum Development.

Brown, R. (1989). Testing and thoughtfulness. *Educational Leadership, 46*(7), 31–33.

Brownlie, F., Close, S. & Wingren, L. (1988). *Reaching for higher thought: Reading, writing, thinking strategies.* Edmonton, Alberta, Canada: Arnold.

Brownlie, F., Close, S. & Wingren, L. (1990). *Tomorrow's classroom today.* Portsmouth, NH: Heinemann.

Burke, K. A. (Ed.). (1992). *Authentic assessment: A collection.* Palatine, IL: IRI/Skylight Publishing.

Burke, K. A. (1997). *Designing professional portfolios for change training manual.* Palatine, IL: IRI/SkyLight Publishing.

Burke, K. A. (1999). *The mindful school: How to assess authentic learning training manual* (3rd ed.). Arlington Heights, IL: SkyLight Training and Publishing.

Burke, K. A. (2000). *What to do with the kid who . . .: Developing cooperation, self-discipline, and responsibility in the classroom.* Arlington Heights, IL: SkyLight Professional Development.

Burke, K. A., Fogarty, R. & Belgrad, S. (2004). *The portfolio connection training manual* (2nd ed.). Glenview, IL: Pearson Professional Development.

Burke, K. A., Fogarty, R. & Belgrad, S. (2002). *The portfolio connection: Student work linked to standards* (2nd ed.). Arlington Heights, IL: SkyLight Professional Development.

Bush, G. W. (2002). *No child left behind act of 2001.* Washington, D.C.: U.S. Department of Education, Office of the Secretary.

Campbell, J. (1992). Laser disk portfolios: Total child assessment. *Educational Leadership, 49*(8), 69–70.

Carr, J. F. & Harris, D. E. (2001). *Succeeding with standards: Linking curriculum, assessment, and action planning.* Alexandria, VA: Association for Supervision and Curriculum Development.

Chapman, C. (1993). *If the shoe fits. . .: How to use multiple intelligences in the classroom.* Palatine, IL: IRI/Skylight Publishing.

Cohen, M. (1980). *First grade takes a test.* New York: Dell Young Yearling, Bantam Doubleday Dell.

Cohen, D. K. (1995). What standards for national standards? *Phi Delta Kappan, 76,* 751–757.

College Entrance Examination Board (1989). *National report on college-bound seniors.* New York: Educational Testing Service.

Combs, A. W. (1976). What we know about learning and criteria for practice. Adapted from a speech at the First National Conference on Grading Alternatives, Cleveland, OH. In S. B. Simon & J. A. Bellanca. *Degrading the grading myths: A primer of alternatives to grades and marks* (pp. 6–9). Alexandria, VA: Association for Supervision and Curriculum Development.

Commission on Chapter 1. (1992). *Making schools work for children in poverty: A new framework prepared by the Commission on Chapter 1.* Baltimore, MD: Author. (ERIC Document Reproduction Service No. ED362618)

Conner, K., Hairston, J., Hill, I., Kopple, H., Marshall, J., Scholnick, K. & Schulman, M. (1985). Using formative testing at the classroom, school and district levels. *Educational Leadership, 43*(2), 63–67.

Conzemius, A. & O'Neill, J. (2001). *Building shared responsibility for student learning.* Alexandria, VA: Association for Supervision and Curriculum Development.

Costa, A. L. (1991). *The school as a home for the mind: A collection of articles.* Palatine, IL: IRI/Skylight Publishing.

Costa, A. L., Bellanca, J. A. & Fogarty, R. (Eds.). (1992a). *If minds matter: A foreword to the future, Volume I.* Palatine, IL: IRI/Skylight Publishing.

Costa, A. L., Bellanca, J. A. & Fogarty, R. (Eds.). (1992b). *If minds matter: A foreword to the future, Volume II.* Palatine, IL: IRI/Skylight Publishing.

Costa, A. L. & Kallick, B. (1992). Reassessing assessment. In A. L. Costa, J. A. Bellanca & R. Fogarty (Eds.), *If minds matter: A foreword to the future, Volume II* (pp. 275–280). Palatine, IL: IRI/Skylight Publishing.

Cross, C. T. (1998). The standards wars: Some lessons learned. *Education Week, 18*(8), 32–35.

Danielson, C. (1997). *A collection of performance tasks and rubrics: Middle school mathematics.* Larchmont, NY: Eye on Education.

Darling-Hammond, L. (1997). *The right to learn: A blueprint for creating schools that work.* San Francisco: Jossey-Bass.

Darling-Hammond, L. & Falk, B. (1997). Using standards and assessments to support student learning. *Phi Delta Kappan, 79*(3), 190.

de Bono, E. (1992). *Serious creativity.* New York: HarperCollins.

DeMott, B. (1990). Why we read and write. *Educational Leadership, 47*(6), 6.

Dewey, J. (1938). *Experience and education.* New York: Macmillan.

Diez, M. E. & Moon, C. J. (1992). What do we want students to know? And other important questions. *Educational Leadership, 49*(8), 38–41.

Drummond, M. J. (1994). *Learning to see: Assessment through observation.* Markham, Ontario, Canada: Pembroke.

Educators in Connecticut's Pomperaug Regional School District 15. (1996). *A teacher's guide to performance-based learning and assessment.* Alexandria, VA: Association for Supervision and Curriculum Development.

Eisner, E. W. (1993). Why standards may not improve schools. *Educational Leadership, 50*(5), 22–23.

Eisner, E. W. (1994). *Cognition and curriculum reconsidered* (2nd ed.). New York: Teachers College, Columbia University.

References

Eisner, E. W. (1995). Standards for American schools: Help or hindrance? *Phi Delta Kappan, 76*(10), 758–764.

Elmore, R. F. (2002). Bridging the gap between standards and achievement: The imperative for professional development in education. Washington, DC: Author. (ERIC Document Reproduction Service No. ED475871)

Farr, B. P. & Trumbull, T. (Eds.). (1997). *Assessment alternatives for diverse classrooms.* Norwood, MA: Christopher-Gordon.

Ferrara, S. & McTighe, J. (1992). Assessment: A thoughtful process. In A. L. Costa, J. A. Bellanca & R. Fogarty (Eds.), *If minds matter: A foreword to the future, Volume II* (pp. 337–348). Palatine, IL: IRI/Skylight Publishing.

Fogarty, R. (1992a). Teaching for transfer. In A. L. Costa, J. A. Bellanca & R. Fogarty (Eds.), *If minds matter: A foreword to the future, Volume I* (pp. 211–223). Palatine, IL: IRI/Skylight Publishing.

Fogarty, R. (1992b). The most significant outcome. In A. L. Costa, J. A. Bellanca & R. Fogarty (Eds.), *If minds matter: A foreword to the future, Volume II* (pp. 349–354). Palatine, IL: IRI/ Skylight Publishing.

Fogarty, R. (2002). *Brain-compatible classrooms.* Arlington Heights, IL: SkyLight Professional Development.

Fogarty, R. & Bellanca, J. A. (1987). *Patterns for thinking: Patterns for transfer.* Palatine, IL: IRI/ Skylight Publishing.

Fogarty, R., Perkins, D. & Barell, J. (1992). *The mindful school: How to teach for transfer.* Palatine, IL: IRI/Skylight Publishing.

Fogarty, R. & Stoehr, J. (1995). *Integrating curricula with multiple intelligences: Teams, themes, and threads.* Arlington Heights, IL: IRI/Skylight Training and Publishing.

Frazier, D. M. & Paulson, F. L. (1992). How portfolios motivate reluctant writers. *Educational Leadership, 49*(8), 62–65.

Foriska, T. J. (1998). *Restructuring around standards: A practitioner's guide to design and implementation.* Thousand Oaks, CA: Corwin Press.

Frender, G. (1990). *Learning to learn: Strengthening study skills and brain power.* Nashville, TN: Incentive.

Fusco, E. & Fountain, G. (1992). Reflective teacher, reflective learner. In A. L. Costa, J. A. Bellanca & R. Fogarty (Eds.), *If minds matter: A foreword to the future, Volume I* (pp. 239–255). Palatine, IL: IRI/Skylight Publishing.

Gandal, M. & Vranek, J. (2001). Standards: Here today, here tomorrow. *Educational Leadership, 59*(1), 7–13.

Gardner, H. (1983). *Frames of mind: The theory of multiple intelligences.* New York: Basic.

Gardner, H. (1991). *Intelligences in seven phases.* Paper presented at the 100th Anniversary of Education at Harvard, Cambridge, MA.

Gentile, J. R. & Lalley, J. P. (2003). *Standards and mastery learning: Aligning teaching and assessment so all children can learn.* Thousand Oaks, CA: Corwin Press.

Glasser, W. (1990). *Quality school: Managing students without coercion.* New York: Harper Perennial.

Glasser, W. (1986). *Control theory in the classroom.* New York: Harper and Row.

Glazer, S. M. & Brown, C. S. (1993). *Portfolios and beyond: Collaborative assessment in reading and writing.* Norwood, MA: Christopher-Gordon.

Goleman, D. (1995). *Emotional intelligence: Why it can matter more than IQ.* New York: Bantam Books.

Goodlad, J. I. (1994). *A place called school.* New York: McGraw-Hill.

Gregory, G. H. & Chapman, C. (2002). *Differentiated instructional strategies: One size doesn't fit all.* Thousand Oaks, CA: Corwin Press.

Gregory, G. H. & Kuzmich, L. (2004). *Data-driven differentiation in the standards-based classroom.* Thousand Oaks, CA: Corwin Press.

Gronlund, N. E. (1998). *Assessment of student achievement* (6th ed.). Boston: Allyn and Bacon.

Guskey, T. R. (Ed.). (1994). *High-stakes performance assessment: Perspectives on Kentucky's educational reform.* Thousand Oaks, CA: Corwin Press.

Guskey, T. R. (Ed.). (1996). *ASCD yearbook 1996: Communicating student learning.* Alexandria, VA: Association for Supervision and Curriculum Development.

Guskey, T. R. (2001). Helping standards make the grade. *Educational Leadership, 59*(1), 20–27.

Guskey, T. R. (2003). How classroom assessments improve learning. *Educational Leadership, 60*(5), 6–11.

Hamm, M. & Adams, D. (1991). Portfolio: It's not just for artists anymore. *Science Teacher, 58*(5), 18–21.

Hammerman, E. & Musial, D. (1995). *Classroom 2061: Activity-based assessments in science.* Arlington Heights, IL: IRI/SkyLight Training and Publishing.

Hansen, J. (1992). Literacy portfolios: Helping students know themselves. *Educational Leadership, 49*(8), 66–68.

Harp, B. (Ed.). (1994). *Assessment and evaluation for student-centered learning. Expanded Professional Version* (2nd ed.). Norwood, MA: Christopher-Gordon.

Harrington-Lueker, D. (1998). States raise the bar. Now local school districts are accountable for results. *The American School Board Journal, 185*(6), 17–21.

Harris, D. E. & Carr, J. F. (1996). *How to use standards in the classroom.* Alexandria, VA: Association for Supervision and Curriculum Development.

Hebert, E. (1992). Portfolios invite reflection—From students and staff. *Educational Leadership, 49*(8), 58–61.

Herman, J. L. (1992). What research tells us about good assessment. *Educational Leadership, 49*(8), 74–78.

Herman, J. L., Aschbacher, P. R. & Winters, L. (1992). *A practical guide to alternative assessment.* Alexandria, VA: Association for Supervision and Curriculum Development.

Hetterscheidt, J., Pott, L., Russell, K. & Tchang, J. (1992). Using the computer as a reading portfolio. *Educational Leadership, 49*(8), 73.

Hibbard, K. M. & Wagner, E. A. (2003). *Assessing and teaching: Reading comprehension and writing, K–3, Volume 2.* Larchmont, NY: Eye on Education.

Hills, J. R. (1991). Apathy concerning grading and testing. *Phi Delta Kappan, 72*(7), 540–545.

Hodgkinson, H. (1991). Reform versus reality. *Phi Delta Kappan, 73*(1), 8–16.

Hyerle, D. (1996). *Visual tools for constructing knowledge.* Alexandria, VA: Association for Supervision and Curriculum Development.

Illinois State Board of Education. (1997). *Illinois learning standards* (adopted July 25, 1997). Springfield, IL: Author.

References

Jacob, B. A. (2001). Getting tough? The impact of high school graduation exams. *Educational Evaluation and Policy Analysis, 23*(2), 99–121.

Jensen, E. (1998). How Julie's brain learns. *Educational Leadership, 6*(3), 43.

Jeroski, S. (1992). Finding out what we need to know. In A. L. Costa, J. A. Bellanca & R. Fogarty (Eds.), *If minds matter: A foreword to the future, Volume II* (pp. 281–295). Palatine, IL: IRI/Skylight Publishing.

Jeroski, S. & Brownlie, F. (1992). How do we know we're getting better? In A. L. Costa, J. A. Bellanca & R. Fogarty (Eds.), *If minds matter: A foreword to the future, Volume II* (pp. 321–336). Palatine, IL: IRI/Skylight Publishing.

Jeroski, S., Brownlie, F. & Kaser, L. (1990a). *Reading and responding: Evaluating resources for your classroom: 1–3, Grades 4–6.* Toronto, Ontario, Canada: Nelson Canada. (Available in the U.S. from The Wright Group, Bothel, WA.)

Jeroski, S., Brownlie, F. & Kaser, L. (1990b). *Reading and responding: Evaluation resources for your classroom: 1–2, Late primary and primary.* Toronto, Ontario, Canada: Nelson Canada. (Available in the U.S. from The Wright Group, Bothel, WA.)

Jervis, K. (1989). Daryl takes a test. *Educational Leadership, 46*(7), 93–98.

Johnson, B. (1992, Winter). Creating performance assessments. *Holistic Educational Review,* pp. 38–44.

Johnson, N. J. & Rose, L. M. (1997). *Portfolios: Clarifying, constructing, and enhancing.* Lancaster, PA: TECHNOMIC.

Johnson, R. S. (2002). *Using data to close the achievement gap: How to measure equity in our schools* (2nd ed.). Thousand Oaks, CA: Corwin Press.

Joint Committee on Standards for Education Evaluation., A. R. Gullickson, chair. (2003). *The student evaluation standards: How to improve evaluations of students.* Thousand Oaks, CA: Corwin Press.

Jones, B. F., Palincsar, A. S., Ogle, D. S. & Carr, E. G. (Eds.). (1987). *Strategic teaching and learning: Cognitive instruction in the content areas.* Alexandria, VA: Association for Supervision and Curriculum Development.

Kallick, B. (1992). Evaluation: A collaborative process. In A. L. Costa, J. A. Bellanca & R. Fogarty (Eds.), *If minds matter: A foreword to the future, Volume II* (pp. 313–319). Palatine, IL: IRI/Skylight Publishing.

Kendall, J. S. & Marzano, R. J. (1997). *Content knowledge: A compendium of standards and benchmarks for K–12 education* (2nd ed.). Aurora, CO: Mid-Continent Regional Educational Laboratory (MCREL); Alexandria, VA: Association for Supervision and Curriculum Development.

King, J. A. & Evans, K. M. (1991). Can we achieve outcome-based education? *Educational Leadership, 49*(2), 73–75.

Knight, P. (1992). How I use portfolios in mathematics. *Educational Leadership, 49*(8), 71–72.

Kohn, A. (1992). *No contest: The case against competition* (rev. ed.). Boston: Houghton Mifflin.

Kohn, A. (1991) Caring kids: The role of the school. *Phi Delta Kappan, 72*(7), 496–506.

Krogness, M. M. (1991). A question of values. *English Journal, 80*(6), 28–33.

Krynock, K. & Robb, L. (1999). Problem solved: How to coach cognition. *Educational Leadership, 57*(3), 29–32.

Langer, G. M., Colton, A. B. & Goff, L. S. (2003). *Collaborative analysis of student work.* Alexandria, VA: Association for Supervision and Curriculum Development.

Larter, S. & Donnelly, J. (1993). Toronto's benchmark programs. *Educational Leadership, 50*(5), 59–62.

Lazear, D. (1999). *Eight ways of knowing: Teaching for multiple intelligences* (3rd ed.). Arlington Heights, IL: SkyLight Training and Publishing.

Lazear, D. (2003). *Eight ways of teaching: The artistry of teaching with multiple intelligences* (4th ed.). Glenview, IL: SkyLight Professional Development.

Levin, H. M. (1998). Educational performance standards and the economy. *Educational Researcher, 27*(4), 4–10.

Lewin, L. & Shoemaker, B. J. (1998). *Great performances: Creating classroom-based assessment tasks.* Alexandria, VA: Association for Supervision and Curriculum Development.

Madaus, G. F. & Kellaghan, T. (1993). The British experience with "authentic" testing. *Phi Delta Kappan, 74*(6), 458–69, 462–63, 466–69.

Majesky, D. (1993, April.). Grading should go. *Educational Leadership,* pp. 88–90.

Malarz, L., D'Arcangelo, M. & Kiernan, L. J. (1991). *Redesigning assessment: Introduction. Facilitator's Guide.* Alexandria, VA: Association for Supervision and Curriculum Development.

Martin-Kniep, G. O. (2000). *Becoming a better teacher: Eight innovations that work.* Alexandria, VA: Association for Supervision and Curriculum Development.

Marzano, R. J. (2003a). Using data: Two wrongs and a right. *Educational Leadership, 60*(5), 32–38.

Marzano, R. J. (2003b). *What works in schools: Translating research into action.* Alexandria, VA: Association for Supervision and Curriculum Development.

Marzano, R. J. & Costa, A. L. (1988). Question: Do standardized tests measure general cognitive skills? Answer: No. *Educational Leadership, 45*(8), 66–71.

Marzano, R. J. & Kendall, J. S. (1996). *A comprehensive guide to designing standards-based districts, schools, and classrooms.* Alexandria, VA: Association for Supervision and Curriculum Development; Aurora, CO: Mid-Continent Regional Educational Laboratory.

Marzano, R. J., Marzano, J. S. & Pickering, D. J. (2003). *Classroom management that works: Research-based strategies for every teacher.* Alexandria, VA: Association for Supervision and Curriculum Development.

Marzano, R. J., Pickering, D. & McTighe, J. (1993). *Assessing student outcomes: Performance assessment using the dimensions of learning model.* Alexandria, VA: Association for Supervision and Curriculum Development.

Marzano, R., Pickering, D. & Pollock, J. (2005). *Classroom instruction that works: Research-based strategies for increasing student achievement.* Boston: Allyn and Bacon.

Maslow, A. H. (1971). Peak experiences in education and art. *Theory into Practice, 10*(3), 149–153.

McKeown, M. G. & Beck, I. L. (1999). Getting the discussion started. *Educational Leadership, 57*(3), 25–28.

McTighe, J. & Lyman, F. T. (1992). Mind tools for matters of the mind. In A. L. Costa, J. A. Bellanca & R. Fogarty (Eds.), *If minds matter: A foreword to the future, Volume II* (pp. 71–90). Palatine, IL: IRI/Skylight Publishing.

Mehrens, W. A. (1992). Using performance assessment for accountability purposes. *Educational Measurement: Issues and Practices, 11*(1), 3–9.

Messacappa, D. (1998). A lesson in mediocrity: How teachers are trained and chosen. *Philadelphia Inquirer,* p. A01. Available online at http://hart.camden.rutgers.edu/adolescence/inthe.htm.

References

Ministry of Education, Province of British Columbia. (1991a). *Enabling learners: Year 2000: A framework for learning.* Author.

Ministry of Education, Province of British Columbia. (1991b). *Supporting learning: Understanding and assessing the progress of children in the primary program: A resource for parents and teachers.* Author.

Moye, V. H. (1997). *Conditions that support transfer for change.* Arlington Heights, IL: IRI/SkyLight Training and Publishing.

NASSP's Council on Middle Level Education. (1988). *Assessing excellence: A guide for studying the middle level school.* Reston, VA: National Association of Secondary School Principals.

National Commission on Excellence in Education. (1983). *A nation at risk: The imperative for educational reform.* (A report to the nation and the Secretary of Education, United States Department of Education). Washington, DC: Author.

Noddings, N. (1997). Thinking about standards. *Phi Delta Kappan, 79*(3), 184.

North Central Regional Educational Laboratory (NCREL). (1991a). *Schools that work: The research advantage. (Guidebook No. 4, Alternatives for Measuring Performance).* Oak Brook, IL: Author.

North Central Regional Educational Laboratory (NCREL). (1991b). *Alternative assessment: Policy beliefs. (Guidebooks No. 15 & 16).* Oak Brook, IL: Author.

Oakes, J. (1989). What educational indicators?: The case for assessing the school context. *Educational Evaluation and Policy Analysis, 11,* 182.

O'Connor, K. (2002). *How to grade for learning: Linking grades to standards* (2nd ed.). Arlington Heights, IL: SkyLight Professional Development.

Ogle, D. M. (1986). K-W-L: A teaching model that develops active reading of expository text. *Reading Teacher, 39*(6), 564–570.

O'Neil, J. (1992). Putting performance assessment to the test. *Educational Leadership, 49*(8), 14–19.

Paulson, F. L., Paulson, P. R. & Meyer, C. A. (1991). What makes a portfolio a portfolio? *Educational Leadership, 48*(5), 60–63.

Perkins, D. & Salomon, G. (1992). The science and art of transfer. In A. L. Costa, J. A. Bellanca & R. Fogarty (Eds.), *If minds matter: A foreword to the future, Volume I* (pp. 201–209). Palatine, IL: IRI/Skylight Publishing.

Perrone, V. (Ed.). (1991). *Expanding student assessment.* Alexandria, VA: Association for Supervision and Curriculum Development.

Pete, B. & Fogarty, R. (2003). *Nine "best practices" that make a difference.* Chicago, IL: Robin Fogarty and Associates.

Pipho, C. (1990). Stateline: Budgets, politics, and testing. *Phi Delta Kappan, 72*(2), 102–103.

Pipho, C. (1992). Stateline: Outcomes or "Edubabble"? *Phi Delta Kappan, 73*(9), 662–663.

Popham, W. J. (1999). *Classroom assessment: What teachers need to know* (2nd ed.). Boston: Allyn and Bacon.

Popham, W. J. (2001). Teaching to the test? *Educational Leadership,* 58(6), 16–20.

Purves, A. C., Quattrini, J. A. & Sullivan, C. I. (1995). *Creating the writing portfolio: A guide to students.* Lincolnwood, IL: NTC Publishing Group.

Ravitch, D. (1995). *National standards in American education: A citizen's guide.* Washington, D.C.: Brookings Institution Press.

Redding, N. (1992). Assessing the big outcomes. *Educational Leadership, 49*(8), 49–51, 53.

Rhoades, J. & McCabe, M. (1992). Cognition and cooperation: Partners in excellence. In A. L. Costa, J. A. Bellanca & R. Fogarty (Eds.), *If minds matter: A foreword to the future, Volume II* (pp. 43–51). Palatine, IL: IRI/Skylight Publishing.

Richetti, C. & Sheerin, J. (1999). Helping students ask the right questions. *Educational Leadership, 57*(3), 58–62.

Rolheiser, C., Bower, B. & Stevahn, L. (2000). *The portfolio organizer: Succeeding with portfolios in your classroom.* Alexandria, VA: Association for Supervision and Curriculum Development.

Rowe, M. B. (1974). Reflections on wait-time: Some methodological questions. *Journal of Research in Science Teaching, 11*(3), 263–279.

Sagor, R. (2003). *Motivating students and teachers in an era of standards.* Alexandria, VA: Association for Supervision and Curriculum Development.

Scherer, M. (Ed.). (1999). The understanding pathway: A conversation with Howard Gardner. *Educational Leadership, 57*(3), 12–16.

Scherer, M. (2001). How and why standards can improve student achievement: A conversation with Robert J. Marzano. *Educational Leadership, 59*(1), 14–18.

Scherer, M. (2002). Do students come about learning?: A conversation with Mihaly Czikszentmihaly. *Educational Leadership, 60*(1), 12–17.

Schmoker, M. (1996). *Results: The key to continuous school improvement.* Alexandria, VA: Association for Supervision and Curriculum Development.

Schmoker, M. (2001). *The results field book: Practical strategies from dramatically improved schools.* Alexandria, VA: Association for Supervision and Curriculum Development.

Schudson, M. (1972). Organizing the 'meritocracy': A history of the College Entrance Examination Board. *Harvard Educational Review, 42*(1), 40–69.

Secretary's Commission on Achieving Necessary Skills (SCANS). (1991). *What work requires of schools: A SCANS report for America 2000.* Washington, D.C.: United States Department of Labor, SCANS.

Secretary's Commission on Achieving Necessary Skills (SCANS). (1992). *Learning a living: A blueprint for high performance: A SCANS report for America 2000.* Washington, D.C.: United States Department of Labor, SCANS.

Semple, B. M. (1992). *Performance assessment: An international experiment.* Princeton, NJ: Educational Testing Service.

Shaklee, B. D., Barbour, N. E., Ambrose, R. & Hansford, S. J. (1997). *Designing and using portfolios.* Boston: Allyn and Bacon.

Shavelson, R. S. & Baxter, G. P. (1992). What we've learned about assessing hands-on science. *Educational Leadership, 49*(8), 20–25.

Shepard, L. (1989). Why we need better assessments. *Educational Leadership, 46*(7), 4–9.

Shepard, L. & Smith, M. L. (1986). Synthesis of research on school readiness and kindergarten retention. *Educational Leadership, 44*(3), 78–86.

Shulman, L. (1988). A union of insufficiencies: Strategies for teacher assessment in a period of reform. *Educational Leadership, 46*(3), 36–41.

Simmons, W. & Resnick, L. (1993). Assessment as the catalyst of school reform. *Educational Leadership, 50*(5), 11–15.

References

Simon, S. B. & Bellanca, J. A. (Eds.). (1976). *Degrading the grading myths: A primer of alternatives to grades and marks*. Washington, D.C.: Association for Supervision and Curriculum Development.

Sizer, T. R. & Rogers, B. (1993). Designing standards: Achieving the delicate balance. *Educational Leadership, 50*(5), 24–26.

Solomon, P. G. (1998). *The curriculum bridge: From standards to actual classroom practice*. Thousand Oaks, CA: Corwin Press.

Solomon, P. G. (2002). *The assessment bridge: Positive ways to link tests to learning, standards, and curriculum improvement*. Thousand Oaks, CA: Corwin Press.

Sousa, D. A. (1995). *How the brain learns*. Reston, VA: National Association of Secondary School Principals.

Sousa, D. A. (2001). *How the brain learns*. (2nd ed.). Thousand Oaks, CA: Corwin Press.

Spady, W. G. & Marshall, K. J. (1991). Beyond traditional outcome-based education. *Educational Leadership, 49*(2), 67–72.

Stefonek, T. (1991). *Alternative assessment: A national perspective: Policy Briefs No. 15 & 16*. Oak Brook, IL: North Central Regional Educational Laboratory.

Stiggins, R. J. (1985). Improving assessment where it means the most: In the classroom. *Educational Leadership, 43*(2), 69–74.

Stiggins, R. J. (1991). Assessment literacy. *Phi Delta Kappan, 72*(7), 534–539.

Stiggins, R. J. (1994). *Student-centered classroom assessment*. New York: MacMillan College Publishing.

Stiggins, R. J. (2002). Assessment crisis: The absence of assessment for learning. *Phi Delta Kappan, 83*(10), 758–765.

Strong, R. W., Silver, H. F. & Perini, M. J. (2001). *Teaching what matters most: Standards and strategies for raising student achievement*. Alexandria, VA: Association for Supervision and Curriculum Development.

Szetela, W. & Nicol, C. (1992). Evaluating problem solving in mathematics. *Educational Leadership, 49*(8), 42–45.

Taggart, G. L., Phifer, S. J., Nixon, J. A. & Wood, M. (Eds.) (1998). *Rubrics: A handbook for construction and use*. Lancaster, PA: TECHNOMIC.

Thornburg, D. D. (2002). *The new basics: Education and the future of work in the telematic age*. Alexandria, VA: Association for Supervision and Curriculum Development.

Tierney, R. J., Carter, M. A. & Desai, L. E. (1991). *Portfolio assessment in the reading writing classroom*. Norwood, MA: Christopher-Gordon.

Tomlinson, C. A. (1999). *The differentiated classroom: Responding to the needs of all learners*. Alexandria, VA: Association for Supervision and Curriculum Development.

Tomlinson, C. A. (2001). Grading for success. *Educational Leadership, 58*(6), 12–15.

Tomlinson, C. A. (2002). Invitations to learn. *Educational Leadership, 60*(1), 6–10.

Tomlinson, C. A. (2003). *Fulfilling the promise of the differentiated classroom: Strategies and tools for responsive teaching*. Alexandria, VA: Association for Supervision and Curriculum Development.

Tomlinson, C. A. & Eidson, C. C. (2003). *Differentiation in practice: A resource guide for differentiating curriculum, Grades K–5*. Alexandria, VA: Association for Supervision and Curriculum Development.

Tyler, R. W. (1949). *Basic principles of curriculum and instruction.* Chicago: University of Chicago Press.

US Department of Labor. (1992). *Learning a living: A blueprint for high performance. (A SCANS report for America 2000).* Washington, D.C.: The Secretary's Commission on Achieving Necessary Skills.

Vacca, R. T. (2002). From efficient decoders to strategic readers. *Educational Leadership, 60*(3), 7–11.

Vavrus, L. (1990). Put portfolios to the test. *Instructor, 100*(1), 48–53.

Vickery, T. R. (1988). Learning from an outcomes-driven school district. *Educational Leadership, 45*(5), 52–56.

Wandt, E. & Brown, G. (1957). *Essentials of educational evaluation.* New York: Holt, Rinehart, and Winston.

White, N., Blythe, T. & Gardner, H. (1992). Multiple intelligences theory: Creating the thoughtful classroom. In A. L. Costa, J. A. Bellanca & R. Fogarty (Eds.), *If minds matter: A foreword to the future, Volume II* (pp. 127–134). Palatine, IL: IRI/Skylight Publishing.

Wiggins, G. (1989). Teaching to the (authentic) test. *Educational Leadership, 46*(7), 41–47.

Wiggins, G. (1992). Creating tests worth taking. *Educational Leadership, 49*(8), 26–33.

Wiggins, G. (1998). *Educative assessment: Designing assessments to inform and improve student performance.* San Francisco: Jossey-Bass.

Wiggins, G. & McTighe, J. (1998). *Understanding by design.* Alexandria, VA: Association for Supervision and Curriculum Development (44).

Williams, B. (Ed.). (1996). *Closing the achievement gap: A vision for changing beliefs and practices.* Alexandria, VA: Association for Supervision and Curriculum Development.

Williams, R. B. (1993). *More than 50 ways to build team consensus.* Palatine, IL: IRI/Skylight Publishing.

Winograd, P. & Gaskins, R. W. (1992). Metacognition: Matters of the mind, matters of the heart. In A. L. Costa, J. A. Bellanca & R. Fogarty (Eds.), *If minds matter: A foreword to the future, Volume I* (pp. 225–238). Palatine, IL: IRI/Skylight Publishing.

Wolf, D. P. (1989). Portfolio assessment: Sampling student work. *Educational Leadership, 46*(7), 35–39.

Wolf, D. P., LeMahieu, P. G. & Eresh, J. (1992, May). Good measure: Assessment as a tool for educational reform. *Educational Leadership,* pp. 8–13.

Wolfe, P. & Brandt, R. (1998). What do we know from brain research? *Educational Leadership, 56*(3), 8–13.

Wolk, R. A. (1998). Commentary: Education's high-stake gamble. *Education Week, 18*(15), 48.

World-Class Standards . . . For World-Class Kids. (1991). *Information on 1991–1992 Assessments.* Kentucky Department of Education.

Worthen, B. R. (1993). Critical issues that will determine the future of alternative assessment. *Phi Delta Kappan, 74*(6), 444–448, 450–454.

Zemelman, S., Daniels, N. & Hyde, A. (1993). *Best practices: New standards for teaching and learning in America's schools.* Portsmouth, NH: Heinemann.

INDEX

**CORWIN
PRESS**

The Corwin Press logo—a raven striding across an open book—represents the union of courage and learning. Corwin Press is committed to improving education for all learners by publishing books and other professional development resources for those serving the field of K–12 education. By providing practical, hands-on materials, Corwin Press continues to carry out the promise of its motto: **"Helping Educators Do Their Work Better."**